Changing Behaviour at Work

When organizations face problems with costs, quality, productivity and attendance, these problems often stem from ineffective patterns of behaviour that the organization is unwittingly encouraging. To prevent and stop these problems, a behavioural approach to managing people is often the most effective.

Changing Behaviour at Work is a lively textbook that illustrates how behaviour analysis theory can be used to alter the way people behave at work. Showing how managers can identify, measure, analyse and change undesirable behaviour, the book takes a highly practical look at management strategies. The authors use case studies to show how managers can implement effective strategies for change, with examples ranging from behavioural self-management to changing the behaviour of large groups.

Topics covered include:

- brief history of behaviour analysis
- traditional approaches to management
- self-management and management of other individuals
- managing groups
- managing at the organizational level

Offering both a theoretically grounded and highly practical perspective, this is an essential purchase for all those seeking to understand how to manage people and organizations more effectively.

Peter Makin is Course Director for the Manchester Business School's MSc in Organizational Psychology, and also teaches on the part-time MBA in the School. He has carried out consultancy work for numerous organizations. **Charles Cox** was formerly Head of the Psychology Group in the Manchester School of Management. He has worked as a consultant with numerous organizations throughout the world.

Changing Behaviour at Work

A practical guide

Peter Makin and
Charles Cox

Routledge
Taylor & Francis Group

LONDON AND NEW YORK

First published 2004
by Routledge
2 Park Square, Milton Park, Abingdon,
Oxfordshire OX14 4RN

Simultaneously published in the USA and Canada
by Routledge
29 West 35th Street, New York, NY 10001

Routledge is an imprint of the Taylor & Francis Group

Typeset in Perpetua and Bell Gothic by
Keystroke, Jacaranda Lodge, Wolverhampton
Printed and bound in Great Britain by
TJ International Ltd, Padstow, Cornwall

British Library Cataloguing in Publication Data
A catalogue record for this book is available from the British Library

Library of Congress Cataloging in Publication Data
Makin, Peter J.
   Changing behaviour at work : a practical guide / by Peter Makin and Charles Cox.
      p. cm.
   Includes bibliographical references and index.
   1. Industrial management. 2. Organizational change—Management.
   3. Organizational behavior. 4. Psychology, Industrial. 5. Organizational
   effectiveness. I. Cox, Charles. II. Title.
   HD31.M2837 2004
   658.3′001′9—dc22   2004002095

ISBN 0–415–32303–7 (hbk)
ISBN 0–415–32304–5 (pbk)

Dedicated to DKM

Contents

Figures

Tables

Boxes

Glossary

ABC sequence A handy mnemonic for the conditioning process; it stands for Antecedent – Behaviour – Consequences. The antecedent is the cue that initiates the behaviour, which is followed by the consequences. These will give rise to either reinforcement (q.v.), in some form, or to punishment (q.v.), thus determining whether the behaviour will continue or decrease.

Attribution theory In order to operate in the world we need to know what causes the events that concern us. Attribution theory is concerned with how we attribute causes to such events. The theory suggests many types of explanation for the causes of behaviour. Two main, and important, dimensions are whether we attribute behaviour to internal factors (e.g. characteristics of the individual) or external factors (factors in the environment).

Baseline A measure of the existing level of behaviour, before any intervention, usually taken over a period of several weeks. This enables the effect of the intervention to be measured.

Classical conditioning A form of conditioning demonstrated by Ivan Pavlov, consisting of an associative shift of a reflex response to a stimulus (e.g. salivation in response to the smell of food) to a new stimulus (e.g. a bell). After a series of trials in which the bell is rung before presenting food, salivation occurs in response to the bell. In humans it offers a possible explanation for emotional reactions to previously neutral stimuli.

Cognitive dissonance The name given to a theory put forward by Leon Festinger, who suggested that if an individual's attitudes are in conflict with their behaviour (i.e. there is a dissonance between them) they will feel a pressure to bring them into alignment. Most commonly their attitudes change to come into line with their behaviour.

Conditioned response In classical conditioning (q.v.) the name given to the response after the associative shift to the new conditioned stimulus (q.v.) has taken place.

Conditioned stimulus In classical conditioning (q.v.) the name given to the stimulus which elicits the response, previously only elicited by the unconditioned stimulus (q.v.).

Cue An indicator that initiates a particular behaviour. It can take many forms, e.g. a signal such as a bell or light flashing, the activity of someone or a direct instruction. See also ABC sequence.

Differential reinforcement This refers to the situation where reinforcement is given for an action, which takes place in the presence of a particular stimulus. If the stimulus is not present the action is not reinforced.

Discriminant stimulus A cue or stimulus that indicates to the individual what action, or behaviour, to carry out next, i.e. now is the time to do A rather than B or C.

Extinction If behaviour is followed by neither reinforcement nor punishment it will eventually cease. This is referred to as extinction. It is usually the most effective way to remove undesired behaviour.

Fixed interval reinforcement Reinforcement provided at fixed time intervals (e.g. every ten minutes, or every half-hour) provided the specified behaviour has occurred at least once during the interval.

Fixed ratio reinforcement Reinforcement provided in relation to a fixed amount of the specified behaviour (e.g. every ten pulls of the lever, or every twenty).

Learned helplessness A passive acceptance of situations that the individual believes they can do nothing about, although objectively this may not be true. This is thought to be due to the individual generalizing from a possibly unpleasant experience from which they genuinely could do nothing to escape.

Negative reinforcement The removal of something unpleasant consequent on behaviour (e.g. an electric shock ceases when a button is pushed). This will have the effect of reinforcing the behaviour concerned.

Operant conditioning A form of conditioning where behaviour is modified through reinforcement or punishment, as opposed to classical conditioning (q.v.) where a response is elicited by a stimulus.

Pavlovian conditioning Another term, used occasionally, for classical conditioning (q.v.), because it was first demonstrated by Ivan Pavlov.

Positive reinforcement A reward (something nice) consequent on behaviour.

Premack principle The principle that a less preferred task can be reinforced by a more preferred one. If a less preferred task is followed by a preferred one, the less preferred task will normally be finished in less time than if performed in the reverse sequence. Principle originally discovered by David Premack.

Primary reinforcer A reinforcer that fulfils a basic need of the individual, e.g. food or water.

Punishment An unpleasant consequence resulting from behaviour. It will tend to reduce the behaviour on which it is consequent. Punishment usually is only effective as a means of changing behaviour if it occurs immediately and every time the behaviour in question occurs.

Reinforcement A reward or pleasant outcome consequent on behaviour. See also positive and negative reinforcement.

Response The behaviour emitted as the result of a stimulus (q.v.).

Schedules of reinforcement Reinforcement can be provided on one of three possible schedules – fixed interval, fixed ratio and variable ratio (q.v.).

Self-efficacy The term given to denote a person's belief in their ability to plan and execute a course of action to reach a desired end.

Self-serving bias An aspect of attribution theory (q.v.). It refers to the human tendency to take credit for success and blame others for failures.

Shaping Building up more complex behaviour by means of a series of simple steps, each of which is reinforced and established before moving on to the next.

Skinner box Apparatus used in animal experiments in operant conditioning (q.v.), consisting of a box with a lever in one side, which when operated releases a small amount of food or water.

Skinnerian conditioning Alternative term used occasionally for operant conditioning (q.v.), because this form of conditioning was originally defined by B. F. Skinner.

Stimulus An event which impinges on an individual, often producing a response (q.v.).

Token economy Reinforcement provided by tokens which can be exchanged to fulfil primary needs or some other desired good. Money is a widely used form of token economy, but other forms of tokens can be used.

Unconditioned response In classical conditioning (q.v.) refers to the original 'natural' response, which when shifted to the new (conditioned) stimulus becomes the conditioned response.

Unconditioned stimulus In classical conditioning (q.v.) refers to the original 'natural' stimulus which elicited the original unconditioned response (q.v.).

Variable ratio reinforcement Reinforcement provided in a random way so that it is neither related to the amount of behaviour shown nor to time intervals. Normally the most effective way of firmly establishing behaviour, as measured by the time taken to reach extinction when reinforcement ceases.

Chapter 1

History and background

The purpose of this book is to enable you to change people's behaviour to make it more effective, whether it is your own behaviour, that of other individuals, groups of individuals, or even whole organizations. The theory and techniques we will use are referred to as the *behavioural approach*. We will also, occasionally, use ideas taken from other theories where we have found them to be useful and compatible with the behavioural approach.

THE BEHAVIOURAL APPROACH TO MANAGEMENT

What's different about the behavioural approach?

1. It is based on sound psychological theory that has a proven track record.
2. Despite the fact that it is theory-based, the approach is very pragmatic. Rather than deal with the psychological 'causes' of behaviour, like attitudes and personalities, it deals with problem *behaviour* directly.
3. It is very difficult for managers to change attitudes and even more difficult, if not impossible, for them to change someone's personality. *Behaviour*, on the other hand, can be changed using techniques that are relatively easy to learn and apply.
4. We have taught the techniques to hundreds of managers, who have used them to solve a wide range of behavioural problems. These range from individual problems, such as stopping a colleague making derogatory personal comments in front of subordinates, or improving golf putting, to getting a whole factory to behave more safely.

In this chapter we will describe the background to the theory and give a brief historical overview of its place in psychological thinking.

In Chapter 2 we will look at some of the more important and influential 'traditional' approaches to dealing with people problems in order to contrast them with the behavioural approach.

Chapter 3 will then deal with basics of behavioural theory, using examples from work and every-day life to demonstrate the important concepts.

In Chapters 4 to 6 we will show how the theory can be used to change the behaviour of individuals, groups and even organizations. Case studies will be used which, with few exceptions, are drawn from projects carried out by managers we have taught. Additions and extensions to the theory will be introduced where they are appropriate for the case study being described.

The final chapter will deal with the 'mechanics' of how behaviour can be correctly specified and measured. The second part of the chapter will deal with practical problems in behavioural change programmes and how they can be minimized.

Introduction to the behavioural approach

The theory we will be using is part of 'behavioural psychology'. Unfortunately for clarity, the theory is currently in the throes of a name change. Originally the theory was known as *behaviour modification* (BMod for short), which, when applied to organizations became, not surprisingly, *organizational behaviour modification* (OBMod). More recently, possibly because the term 'modification' has overtones of manipulation, some writers have started using the term *behavioural analysis* which, in its applied form, is referred to as *applied behavioural analysis*. (More confusion is also possible because some writers use 'behaviour', rather than 'behaviour*al*'.) Despite this potential confusion, however, the theory remains the same. In fact one important term remains common to both titles – behaviour. The presence of 'behaviour' in both titles is important, for reasons that, we hope, will soon become clear. In this book we will tend to use the terms BMod and OBMod but we may, on occasions, use the alternatives.

Unlike some of the traditional approaches, which we will consider in the next chapter, the behavioural approach does not look for deep, internal, causes of behaviour such as attitudes or personality. Instead it concentrates on the behaviour itself, and on ways of influencing behaviour to bring about the desired change. As we will see, however, getting managers to specify people problems in terms of behaviour is not always easy. An example from the authors' experience will serve to illustrate this.

We were running a management course in a London hotel and, unknown to us, the person putting out the buffet lunch at the back of the room was the hotel's assistant manager. He must have been paying attention to what we were saying because, after the course was over, he approached us for advice about one of his receptionists. This receptionist, he explained, had a prejudice against Arabs, and he wanted advice as to how to stop this racism. It took us some time to get him to see that what he needed to change was not her racism, but her *behaviour*. Her behaviour towards guests of other racial groups was exemplary and what he wanted was for her to display the same behaviour towards his Arab clientele. (The underlying problem of 'racism', whilst to be deplored, is not an issue for the manager, her behaviour whilst at work, on the other hand, is.)

Specifying problems in behavioural terms makes them more amenable to solution. Behaviour can be changed, personalities cannot. We will be showing how this can be done in later chapters. Before moving on, however, it is perhaps worth pointing out some of the additional advantages of specifying problems in behavioural terms.

One advantage is that employees become aware of precisely what behaviour is expected of them. It may be thought that employees are already aware of what behaviour is required, but this is often not the case. This may appear strange, but it is, in our experience, very common. Even 'simple' jobs, such as that of a bartender or cleaner may benefit from an analysis in behavioural terms. It is, for example, often not clear as to whether bartenders, or their managers, are fully aware of what customers expect of a 'good' bartender. Young people, often students, are taken on as bar staff and put behind the bar with little or no instruction as to how to deal with customers. Managers often comment that 'it should be obvious' what is expected of them. One of the authors, tired of poor service, analysed in behavioural terms what customers expected of a 'good' bartender.

Talking to pub customers, it became apparent that one of the main annoyances, especially in crowded pubs, is getting noticed by the bartender so as to be served, hopefully, in your proper place in the queue. Often, in customers' perceptions, the bartender finishes serving a customer and then serves either the person standing immediately behind, or the one who shouts loudest, irrespective of whether or not it was their turn. A specification of the precise behaviours required was, therefore, suggested, that included the following. A good bartender:

1 acknowledges people arriving at the bar for service,
2 indicates to them their place in the queue, and
3 serves them in that order.

This was tried out by one of our post-graduate students who worked part-time in a bar. She followed the behaviours specified above to see what would happen.

Although it was not possible to measure customer satisfaction directly, it was thought that the level of tips would provide an indirect indication of any change. She monitored, therefore, the level of tips before and after the behaviour change. Until she implemented the change her tips had been very close to the average for other staff in the bar. Very shortly after the change was implemented her tips had tripled. The other staff noticed this and wondered what was leading to her enhanced earnings. Because they knew she was doing a Master's degree in psychology they came to the conclusion that she was hypnotizing the customers!

Just the correct specification of behaviour may, therefore, lead to improved performance – the 'clarification effect'. Another, more systematic, example of such effects is provided by Anderson *et al.* (1988), who concentrated on clarifying the tasks required for cleaning a bar. Even before other behavioural techniques were used, the clarification produced by the behavioural specification produced a 13 per cent improvement.

Another advantage is that specifying problems in behavioural terms often avoids negative emotional reactions to criticism. The reason for this is simple. It is very common to criticize people in terms of broad 'personality' categories, as we have noted above.

The danger of phrasing problems in personal, and global, terms is that problems expressed in this way are perceived as threatening. Such global descriptions are perceived as an attack upon the person's identity. If I am described as 'lazy' or 'selfish', for example, I may well resist this description of myself 'as a person' and respond accordingly. Such traits are relatively stable and difficult to change – hence the defensive reaction. If, on the other hand the problem is expressed in specific behavioural terms the threat is much reduced. To be told that what you *did* on a specific occasion made someone else feel under-valued is more useful. You may, for example apologize for the behaviour, explain that it was not what you had intended, and promise that it would not happen again. As another example, we all, on occasion, *behave* stupidly. That does not, however, mean that we are stupid. Interestingly, in their training, teachers are often taught to 'criticize the behaviour, not the child', a technique that parents, and managers, might be well advised to adopt. Concentrating on what people 'do' rather than 'who they are' may help overcome problems more easily.

An interesting example of the way problems may be easier to solve by specifying them in behavioural terms occurred whilst the authors were carrying out some consultancy work. We were making a presentation, on the lines above, of why it was better not to talk about 'personality-type' descriptions of problem. One manager commented that there was one trait that managers had to do something about, because of health and safety implications. The trait he had in mind was 'alcoholism'. It is true that alcoholism presents problems, but the distinction can still be made between traits and behaviour. A person can be an alcoholic (relatively stable trait) but not drink alcohol (specific behaviour). Although neither of the authors has personal experience of Alcoholics Anonymous, it appears that this organization considers this distinction to be very important. When members speak at a meeting they introduce themselves by saying that 'I am an alcoholic, but I haven't had a drink for x weeks/months/years'. The disposition to drink does not necessarily mean that they have to do so.

Even positive generalizations may pose problems, as Carol Dweck (1999) has shown. Her research, and that of her co-researchers, has demonstrated the problems associated with praising children for being 'clever'. Whilst the child is doing well there are no problems. The problems arise when things go wrong, as they inevitably will. When the child is faced with failure, their self-perception of themselves as being 'clever' is threatened. As with personality, there is little one can do to improve one's 'cleverness'. The child may often, therefore, avoid such situations in the future, so as to avoid further threats to their self-image. If, on the other hand, the successes are attributed to 'effort', rather than 'ability', then there is something they can do to improve their future performance.

On the positive side there may also be advantages to specifying the precise behaviour required. For example, a law in England, dating from 1947, does not allow fireman, even if they are part-time, to serve beyond the age of 55. This is, presumably, because a fireman's job is very physical. This has meant, however, that the fire service has lost possible part-time recruits. In one situation a person was turned down because he was

4

too old. This was despite the fact that he was an extremely fit marathon runner. Recruiting on the basis of what someone has to be able to *do*, rather than how old they are, is perhaps more sensible.

Having outlined the behavioural approach, we now briefly describe its short, but influential, history. If you are not interested in this, you can safely skip to the section 'Early behavioural theory'.

A BRIEF HISTORY OF BEHAVIOURAL PSYCHOLOGY

Like all modern sciences, psychology was originally part of philosophy. The experimental approach, which characterizes the 'modern' scientific method, is a relatively recent development, dating arguably from the Renaissance period (from the mid-fifteenth to mid-seventeenth centuries – the long sixteenth century as it has been called).

Originally psychology followed the 'philosophical', i.e. the reflective rather than experimental, approach. In the nineteenth century, however, it moved into experimentation into its unique subject matter – 'the mind'. The earliest experiments, in the 1870s were carried out in the laboratories of Wilhelm Wundt, often called the founding father of modern psychology. In his Leipzig laboratory he carried out experiments using both introspection (which we will consider shortly) and the use of precision instruments. These instruments were used to examine, for example, reaction times, i.e. how long it takes someone to lift their finger from a key once a light comes on.

The other main investigative method used in early psychology was 'introspection' – asking subjects to 'look in' on their own experiences and then to report them, as accurately as they could, to the researcher. People were asked, for example, to report their mental states when they were imaging events, or experiencing various emotions.

Around the start of the twentieth century the introspective technique came under increasing criticism. The problems with it are fairly obvious. How can someone accurately report what they are experiencing, especially whilst they are experiencing it? It is like the old party trick of getting someone to pat their head and, at the same time, rub their tummy in a circular motion. In addition, people may not always be aware of what they are experiencing, or even be innocently mistaken in their reports. For these reasons, and others, there was a move away from introspection as a technique and towards more observable, and hence verifiable, sources of information.

(In passing, it is worth noticing that introspection is still around. As with many theories and techniques, although they may be superseded, they retain an influence in specialist areas. Introspection is still, perhaps, the main technique in psychotherapy. It is difficult to see how it could be otherwise. I am the only person who has direct access to what I am thinking and feeling.)

The move away from introspection came mainly from America. It could be argued that the move was rooted in the Anglo-American philosophical traditions of 'empiricism' and 'pragmatism', and it is interesting that the 'school' of psychology that it spawned was most influential in those cultures. Rather than looking 'inside', the new school looked only at observable behaviour – hence its name 'behaviourism'.

The 'founding father' of the behaviourist school was John B. Watson, an American. In 1913 he published a famous article in which he suggested that introspection should be abandoned and that psychology should concentrate only on observable behaviour. The scientific investigation of the behaviour of the human animal should follow that used in investigating other animals. These animals cannot report their inner states so all that can be studied is what they *do*, i.e. their observable behaviour.

One of the authors of this book was, before he changed careers, in electrical engineering, and found the concept of the 'black box', used in electrical engineering, useful in illustrating one of the central tenets of behaviourism. The 'black box' referred to here, however, is not that carried by aeroplanes. Rather it is a conceptual device used in, for example, electronics.

As most people are aware, much modern electronic equipment is largely based around the Printed Circuit Board, or PCB. These boards contain hundreds of components and each board is constructed to fulfil a particular function. In a television set, for example, there may be a PCB that detects the sound signal, another the picture signal, another that amplifies the sound signal, and so on. Should a fault occur on your set the engineer will first try to identify the PCB that might have failed. The suspect board will then be tested. As we have said, each PCB may contain hundreds of microchips, resistors, capacitors, etc. To test each component on the board would be very time consuming. Each board, therefore, may have a number of test points, which, for simplicity, we will reduce to just one which works as follows. There is an input point, into which the engineer injects a test signal with specific characteristics. There is also an output point at which the engineer can test the signal that emerges. If the input signal does not produce the correct output signal then there is a fault on the PCB. If this is the case the PCB is replaced, and, it is hoped, the fault is cured.

The important thing to note is that the engineer has no knowledge about where the fault lies on the PCB, or even how the PCB works. The PCB, as far as the service engineer is concerned, is a 'black box', into which it is impossible and unnecessary to see. All that needs to be known is what signal should emerge when a test signal is put in. This is the approach taken by the behaviourists.

The human brain is, most probably, the most complex system of which we have knowledge. Even the most sophisticated brain imaging techniques still give only a very crude picture of what is happening inside. The behaviourists, therefore, do not concern themselves with what happens inside the brain/mind. They limit their investigations to what stimuli go in, and what behaviour emerges as a result. Consider the knee-jerk reflex. The tap with the rubber 'hammer' is the stimulus, the knee-jerk the behaviour that emerges. Such behaviours are referred to as 'responses' and, for this reason it is sometimes referred to as Stimulus–Response, or S–R, psychology.

Perhaps the most famous behaviourist psychologist of modern times is the American B. F. (Burrhus Frederick) Skinner, who died in 1990. His systematic experimental approach to animal and human behaviour did much to advance, and make influential, behaviourism as a major school of psychology. Indeed, it could be argued that behaviourism was the dominant school from the 1930s to the 1960s, when the cognitive school replaced it.

We will describe the details of behaviourist theory in Chapter 3. At present, therefore we will refrain from examining its strengths and look instead at two major criticisms of behaviourism that demonstrated its limitations. We will then consider its current status and development.

There are two main criticisms of behaviourism. The first concerns what is happening when we are thinking to ourselves, the second our emotions.

The issue about what behaviour is occurring when we are silently thinking to ourselves is one that has occupied philosophers with a behavioural approach for a long time, with little success. There have been a number of solutions suggested, but one interesting one was that, when we are thinking we are actually engaged in sub-vocal speech. In other words we are talking to ourselves at a level that cannot be heard. This was shown to be false when researchers injected a volunteer with curare, a paralysing drug used by native South Americans. The drug paralysed the volunteer's muscles (a heart–lung machine was used to keep them alive!). When they recovered from the drug they reported that they had been able to think, even though their vocals chords had been paralysed.

This philosophical problem is not, perhaps, as important as the second criticism, which concerns the status of emotions. Emotions are extremely important. They are 'feelings' or, in psychological jargon, 'affective states'. How can behaviourism, considering only objective, observable behaviour, deal with emotional feelings which, by their very nature, are so subjective and 'internal'?

Behaviourism tries to cope with his problem by pointing out that many emotions lead to observable behaviour. We recognize the emotional states of others by observing how they behave. We can tell when someone is angry or sad, for example, by the way they behave. In addition there may be changes to their body's physiology. The classic example is the so-called 'fight or flight' syndrome. When faced with danger the body responds by preparing for action. Adrenalin is released into the blood stream, the blood supply to the visceral organs (the digestive system, etc.) is cut whilst that to the skeletal muscles is increased. As someone has said, when a lion is chasing you, you are not normally concerned with digestion or reproduction!

This attempt to deal with emotions by considering only their overt behavioural manifestation is not, however, entirely satisfactory. Different people express their emotions in different ways. Some angry people may bang the table, others may sit in silence. In addition, the same person may also express their anger in different ways on different occasions, depending upon the situation. The behaviourist explanation of emotions remains an important weakness of the theory. It is a major weakness for 'radical' versions of the theory that allow *only* observable behaviour to count as the legitimate subject of investigation.

7

Despite the fact that behaviourism, in its most radical form, has these weaknesses this does not totally invalidate the theory. As with many theories, whilst it does not provide a comprehensive explanation for all behaviour, it retains its value as being a useful explanation for many behaviours. In addition, more recent modifications to the theory have accepted the importance of 'internal' states as partial determinants of people's behaviour. We will discuss these extensions to the theory in more detail when appropriate.

Early behavioural theory

Behavioural theories are, essentially, theories of how people learn. Despite the claim by some psychologists than some of our behaviour is based on primitive instincts, there is little doubt that most of our behaviour is learned. In behavioural theory such learning is usually referred to as *conditioning*. Historically the first of these theories is *classical conditioning*, and the name most associated with it is that of Ivan Pavlov (for this reason it is sometimes referred to as *Pavlovian* conditioning). Many people, we suspect, will have heard of Pavlov. Indeed the stimulus of the course leader saying 'Pavlov' often leads to the response of 'dogs' or 'dogs salivating' from the other participants – an example, perhaps, of conditioning! Whilst the bare outlines of Pavlov's experiments are known to most people, their significance is often less well known or understood.

Ivan Pavlov (1849–1936) investigated the salivation reflex in dogs. When dogs, or humans for that matter, are presented with food they will salivate. This is a physiological reflex, part of the makeup of the nervous system. The stimulus, the food, produces the reflex of salivation. This does not have to be learned. The stimulus, the food, is therefore termed the *un-conditioned* (or unlearned) *stimulus* (UCS) and the salivation is the *un-conditioned response* (UCR). This can be represented as follows:

$$\Phi$$
$$\text{Food} \xrightarrow{\hspace{3cm}} \text{Salivation}$$
$$\text{UCS} \hspace{5cm} \text{UCR}$$

The Greek letter **Φ** above the line stands for Phi, and is the abbreviation for physiology, showing that the link between the two is a physiological reflex.

Now consider what would happen if bell were sounded near a dog. This might produce a number of responses, such as turning of the head, or possibly a bark. It would almost certainly not, however, lead to salivation. What Pavlov noticed was that, if the sound of a bell was regularly followed by the presentation of food, eventually the sound of the bell *by itself* would lead to salivation. This simple observation earned him a Nobel Prize.

The sound of the bell is a stimulus, which also leads to a response but, in this case the link has to be learned. Both stimulus and response are therefore referred to as *conditioned* (learned) stimulus and response. The bell, the *conditioned stimulus* (CS), produces a *conditioned response* (CR) of salivation. This can be represented as follows:

Bell   ⟶   Salivation
CS   CR

These then are the steps of classical conditioning.

1. Food (UCS) automatically produces a physiological response of salivation (UCR).
2. By constant pairing of the food with the bell, eventually the bell by itself (CS) will produce salivation (CR).
3. The un-conditioned response (UCR) and the conditioned response (CR) are the same, in this case salivation.

Classical conditioning provides a useful explanation for many emotional reactions. Many emotions have physiological effects, for example the 'fight or flight' reaction to fear. This prepares the body for action, for example releasing hormones into the blood, redirecting the blood supply from the visceral organs to skeletal muscles etc. This leads to feelings such as 'butterflies in the stomach'.

Classical conditioning can occur if, at the time the emotion is experienced, there is another, otherwise neutral, stimulus that is also being experienced. On future occasions this stimulus may, by itself, produce the original emotional reaction. For example, when the wife of one of the authors was pregnant and experiencing severe morning sickness, the Beatles song 'Penny Lane' was number one in the charts. Even now, over 30 years later, the first few bars of 'Penny Lane' induce in her feelings of nausea.

Such classically conditioned responses are very common – music, smells, sounds, places, etc. can all produce emotional feelings, both pleasant and unpleasant.

Classical conditioning and phobias

Classical conditioning also provides a partial explanation for some phobias. By association, some previously neutral stimulus may become associated with negative emotions. The person affected will then often avoid the stimulus, thus avoiding the negative feelings. A very mild example of such emotions was provided by a manager on one of our courses. He had been involved in a car accident at a road junction on his normal route to work. Following the accident, every time he drove through the junction he experienced very unpleasant feelings. As a result he had developed an alternative, but longer, route that avoided that junction.

Classical conditioning sees phobias as examples of inappropriate learning. A previously neutral stimulus has become associated with one that produces fear and anxiety.

A phobia is characterized by a very powerful, and *irrational*, fear of something that interferes with a person's normal life. Note the emphasis on the irrational element. There are some things of which it is perfectly rational to be fearful. Also, people may have powerful irrational fears that do not interfere with their normal lives. For example, someone with a phobia about heights can avoid the feeling by avoiding heights. As long

9

Box 1.1:
BEHAVIOURAL TREATMENT OF PHOBIAS

There are a number of behavioural techniques that can be used to treat phobias. These break the link between the phobic stimulus and the anxiety and fear. One of the techniques is traumatic, but quick. The other, which has been shown to be very effective, is slower and less dramatic.

The more dramatic (and traumatic) of the two is *emotional flooding*. In essence this means exposing the person to the object of their fear until the anxiety subsides. The assumption behind this technique is that the anxiety reaction is flooded to such an extent that it is eventually exhausted.

The other technique is essentially fairly simple, but has a long name – *systematic desensitization* using *reciprocal inhibition*. This will be explained by taking the two parts of the name separately. We will take the last part, reciprocal inhibition, first.

Reciprocal inhibition works on the fact that a person cannot be relaxed *and* aroused at the same time. As you will recall from Chapter 1, many emotional reactions are based on interpretations of physiological reactions, e.g. the fight or flight reaction. It is physiologically impossible to be relaxed *and* aroused. The patient is, therefore, taught relaxation techniques, which they will use when faced with the object of their phobia.

The other part of the technique, systematic desensitization, involves drawing up a hierarchy of the fear of the object. For a fear of spiders, for example, the greatest fear may be holding a spider in the hands. Lower down the hierarchy may be a spider on the other side of the room whilst at the bottom of the hierarchy may be a photograph of a spider on the other side of the room.

The patient is presented with the lowest level stimulus whilst, at the same time, using relaxation techniques. Once the patient can face the lowest level of stimulus without anxiety, they move up to the next level in the hierarchy and so on. Hence the *systematic* nature of the desensitization procedure.

This technique can be very effective in treating some phobias.

as their job or life does not involve them having to climb, for example as a fire fighter or roof repairer, then their life will not be greatly affected by this phobia. There are some phobias, however, which are both fairly common, and also have an adverse impact on people's lives. A phobia about flying in aircraft, for example, may severely restrict a person's job and holiday opportunities.

In passing, some psychologists object to the fairly recent habit of adding 'phobia' on to various words so as to indicate an irrational fear or, more commonly, an 'irrational' prejudice. Examples include 'homophobia', 'islamophobia', 'anglophobia', 'francophobia', etc. The reason for the objection is that this use of 'phobia' only reflects one aspect of a 'real' phobia, i.e. the irrational nature of the fear. There are two additional aspects of phobias, however, that are crucial to their definition. Someone with a phobia is usually very aware that their fear is irrational, but this does not stop it. In addition, they would also rather not suffer from it. These two features do not apply to those 'phobias' listed above.

Other phobic reactions such as fear of spiders, flying, open spaces, etc. may have their origins in classical conditioning.

In order to demonstrate the differences between 'traditional' approaches to management and the behavioural approach, in the next Chapter we will look at some of the more important of the former techniques. In Chapter 3 we will return to the behavioural approach and consider the essential aspects of the theory.

CHAPTER SUMMARY

One of the key features of the behavioural approach is that it concentrates on behaviour directly, rather than trying to change personal characteristics, such as personality. Concentrating on behaviour brings some immediate advantages – people become aware of precisely what is expected of them and hence can behave accordingly.

Another of the important elements of behavioural theory is that most behaviour is learnt. Classical conditioning helps explain how previously neutral stimuli, when paired with stimuli that produce physiological reactions, can lead to emotional reactions. Such reactions can sometimes be strong enough to produce phobic responses.

Chapter 2

Traditional approaches to management

THE CASE OF DAVID ROBERTS

David Roberts was a successful middle manager in a large manufacturing company. He was in his mid-thirties and keen and enthusiastic. He had attended management courses and read many of the recommended texts and so was familiar with the writings of the currently popular management gurus. As do many managers he felt that much of this was common sense, although some of the more 'far out' ideas did not seem to have much application to his situation. However, he conscientiously tried to apply their recommendations in his daily dealings with his subordinates. Thus he spent time considering how to motivate them and how to improve the attitude of those members of staff who seemed less involved with their work than could be deemed desirable. As a result of his efforts the department ran well and he was respected and generally liked by his staff, nevertheless there were certain problems which did not seem to be solvable. One or two members of staff kept up a steady work pace but no amount of exhortation or driving could increase this, even in emergencies. He had suspicions that one or two others were spending more time chatting with their colleagues than was perhaps desirable, and there was poor old Jim who always seemed to get hold of the wrong end of the stick. However much time he spent on these issues nothing ever seemed to change.

The scenario outlined above is common to many organizations. The problems faced by David Roberts are fairly typical and his method of tackling them is fairly usual, as is his lack of success. In this chapter we will examine why this is, in order to provide a basis for explaining why the behavioural approach can provide better solutions.

How managers manage depends on the beliefs they hold about people and what they believe causes them to behave in any particular way. As McGregor (1960) put it 'every managerial act rests on an assumption'. Although this book was written over forty years ago and the approach is, perhaps, rather simplistic, it still has important implications for management today. For this reason, although the ideas are quite well known, it is worth giving a brief summary for those who have not yet come across them. They are also quite widely misunderstood by those who are only superficially familiar with the theory.

McGregor suggested two possible sets of assumptions that a manager might hold concerning human motivation. He did not suggest that these were the only possible assumptions, but they provided two contrasting views that could then be used to speculate on the likely behaviour of the manager and its effect on the subordinate. To try and avoid value judgements he simply labelled these assumptions *Theory X* and *Theory Y*. The assumption behind Theory X is fairly simple – 'people are basically lazy'; no one would work if they did not have to. Acceptance of this assumption leads to the inevitable conclusion that the only way to get people to work is by using strict control. This control can take two different forms. One way is to use coercion: the threat of punishment if rules are broken or targets not achieved. The alternative approach is to use the 'carrot' rather than the 'stick': people are seduced by promises of rewards into producing the performance required. Theory Y is more difficult to define, partly because it is a more complex set of assumptions, but it involves the notion that people are naturally active, they want to be involved in their work, they enjoy achieving and have the ability and the desire to make a constructive contribution to the solution of any problems that may arise.

If we turn to the likely influence of these two sets of assumptions on a manager's approach to subordinates, it is clear that each will give rise to a very different style of management. Theory X assumptions will lead to close control, involving the setting of precise targets and methods of measuring whether these have been achieved, so that rewards and punishments can be applied. (Readers in the UK may recognize echoes of government policy in areas such as education.) The effect of this on the subordinates is that they feel that they are not trusted, they have no means of making a contribution and are not valued. Since the manager believes them to be lazy and uncommitted any attempt to remonstrate at the system is seen as evidence of their lack of commitment. A common and natural response from subordinates is to simply comply and do what the system requires, this is really their only option. This behaviour will also only serve to confirm the management belief that they are lazy and uninvolved. In other words Theory X assumptions lead almost inevitably to a self-fulfilling prophecy. The managerial behaviours likely to arise from Theory Y assumptions are rather more complex, but are likely to involve greater participation with subordinates in decision making and joint setting of targets. In general, subordinates' skills, abilities and contribution will be valued in a realistic way. What effect this will have on subordinate reactions is more problematic than with Theory X, but it seems more likely to create greater involvement and commitment on the part of subordinates. The main value of McGregor's ideas is that they draw attention very clearly to the effects of manager's assumptions about people. It is important that the two sets of assumptions are only illustrations. Many other, and more complex, sets are actually held by managers. It is also important that this is not a theory of motivation. McGregor was not suggesting that either Theory X or Y is a valid representation of actual human motivation. They are simply beliefs that managers may hold.

13

MANAGERIAL ASSUMPTIONS

Over the years there have been many different sets of assumptions, concerning individual's motivation at work, made by managers (and by consultants and writers on management). These can be a arranged in a rough historical sequence, which is also one of increasing complexity.

1 *Rational / economic motivation* This was very much the prevailing view of the early writers on management; best exemplified by F. W. Taylor, the founder of work study in the 1920s (see Box 2.1). The underlying assumption is that people's motivation is entirely economic and that they are rational in the way they set about fulfilling their financial needs. (Some modern economists still work on rather similar assumptions about behaviour.) The result of these beliefs was so called *scientific management*, where work was carefully designed and scheduled in the 'most efficient' way and then appropriate rates of pay were offered for good

Box 2.1:
F. W. TAYLOR'S SCIENTIFIC MANAGEMENT

Taylor published *The Principles of Scientific Management* in 1911, in which he set out his approach to effective management. This was based on a series of studies of the differences between effective and ineffective workers. In one study, for example, he was able to show that by selecting workers with the right physique and providing the correct design of shovel and appropriate financial incentives, he could considerably increase the amount of pig iron moved during a day. Based on these studies Taylor defined the principles of good man management as consisting in selecting employees with the right skills, providing well-designed tools in the correct working environment and then offering financial incentives for high output. In this rather mechanistic way maximum efficiency would be obtained. He referred to this as *scientific management* because of the emphasis on measurement, prediction and control. This way of thinking still influences modern management in the use of financial incentives and bonus schemes. Also much of personnel selection is based on the mechanistic assumption that it is possible to find a perfect match between the skill requirements of a job and the characteristics of an individual applicant. One slight irony is that although Taylor's original work was entirely at shopfloor level (he saw managerial work as being concerned with thinking rather than physical activity and hence not susceptible to the same techniques), financial incentives now seem to be more widely applied at boardroom level than on the shopfloor.

performance. This is rather like working on Theory X assumptions, since work is carefully prescribed, performance measured and appropriately rewarded. The subordinate has no option but to follow the rules.

2 *Social motivation* The well-known series of experiments carried out in the late 1920s and early 1930s at the Hawthorne plant of the Western Electric Company gave rise to the notion that motivation at work was primarily social, i.e. what motivated people was being part of a team and finding fulfilment through group interaction (see Box 2.2.). This lead to an emphasis in management on designing and rewarding effective work teams. These experiments also gave rise to the phenomena known as the *Hawthorne effect*. This refers to the fact that any change in conditions will often give rise to (at least temporary) improvements in performance, even when there appears to be no logical reason for the change. Often, indeed, performance improves even when physical conditions have got worse, as happened in the Hawthorne experiments. This is important for anyone involved in behaviour change since it is dangerous to assume that any change is because of the nature of your intervention. It may simply be because you intervened.

Box 2.2:
THE HAWTHORNE STUDIES

The 'Hawthorne effect' originated in work done in the USA in the 1920s and 1930s at the Hawthorne works of the Western Electric company (Roethlisberger and Dickson, 1939). The name most commonly associated with the Hawthorne studies is that of Elton Mayo. Although he used much of the data to support his own theories, Mayo himself was never directly involved (Mayo, 1975).

Initially, the researchers were trying to establish the relationship between various physical conditions, such as temperature and lighting, and their effects on productivity. What they found was that there were no consistent relationships. Productivity increased both in the experimental group and in a control group. The level of lighting remained constant for the control group, but was varied in the experimental group. At one point, the level of lighting for the latter was equivalent to that of moonlight. Despite this, productivity did not drop. The researchers eventually concluded that psychological, rather than physical, factors were at work.

The researchers concluded that the increase in productivity was because the workers felt that the researchers were taking an interest in them. The 'Hawthorne effect' has entered sociological and psychological vocabularies; that is, that just observing people will have an effect upon them.

3   *Self-actualization* The writings of Maslow (1954) introduced the idea of human needs beyond those simply for subsistence and belonging, namely esteem and self-actualization (see Box 2.3). In other words, to be highly motivated, people needed to feel that their work is worthwhile and that it contributes to their development. Under these assumptions effective managers have to make sure that their workers understand the importance of their tasks and how they fit into a larger whole, and design work that is meaningful and provides opportunities for development.

4   *Motivation is complex* The reality is, of course, that all the above assumptions can be valid in different circumstances. It may well be that in the 1920s the most pressing need for many people was simply the need to obtain necessities for survival. As economic circumstances improved, other needs, such as affiliation, develop. To be followed later by esteem and self-actualization, as suggested by Maslow's (1954) hierarchy of needs. If motivation is looked at in this way, it becomes obvious that the whole of society is not at the same level at the same time, furthermore any individual will have different needs at different times, or several at the same time. Hence attempting to build management strategies on assumptions about individual needs is a very complex and possibly impossible process.

ATTRIBUTION THEORY

We have seen above how a manager's assumptions about people may well determine his/her approach to managing. This is linked to an aspect of psychology, which goes under the heading of *attribution theory*, which deals specifically with how we attribute causation to events. In order to control our physical environment we need to understand what causes the events in which we are interested. Much of science and technology is concerned with seeking answers to questions of causality. What causes hurricanes, or disease, or cycles of economic activity? However, perhaps the major influence on all our lives is the behaviour of other people. Much management activity is concerned with attempts to control such behaviour, hence our need to try and understand its causes.

Attribution theory suggests that there are two main types of explanation for the causes of behaviour. This is the case whether we are considering management or any other context. The first of these two types of explanation is one that is accepted, almost without question, by the 'man in the street'. It is that a person's behaviour is caused by characteristics such as their personality or their attitudes. Thus accidents, for example, are perceived as being caused by people being 'accident-prone', 'foolhardy', or 'negligent'. In attribution theory terms these explanations are referred to as *internal* attributions because they refer to internal characteristics of the individual concerned. Contrast this sort of internal explanation with the second type. This sees behaviour as being caused not by internal, but rather by *external* factors. Because, as we will see, there is a strong tendency for us to prefer explanations of the first type, we will consider a little further the explanation of behaviour as being externally caused.

16

Box 2.3:
MASLOW'S HIERARCHY OF NEEDS

Maslow (1971) identified five levels of human needs, namely:

1 physiological needs
2 safety needs
3 social needs
4 self-esteem needs
5 self-actualization.

He also proposed that these needs are organized into a hierarchy, usually represented as a pyramid (see diagram below), which indicates that the lower-level needs have to be satisfied before the individual becomes interested in needs at a higher level. Thus someone who is hungry (a physiological need) will only be motivated by food and will not be interested in higher-order needs. When the individual's basic physiological needs are satisfied they become interested in security. Only when secure do they become concerned with belonging. When sure that they belong, status becomes important, and finally they become concerned with self-actualization or achieving their full potential.

At one time, the theory achieved considerable popularity with managers, probably because it has considerable intuitive appeal and helped to clarify what sort of incentives would be most effective in a given context. It is, for example, not much of an incentive to offer long-term security to someone who already feels secure. Many organizations also adopted a strategy based on making sure that lower-level needs were met so that individuals were motivated by self-development and a need to achieve. The assumption being that this would be a powerful motivator and would be open ended, in the sense that it would never be totally fulfilled, thus providing a long-term incentive.

Unfortunately, a lot of real life data does not support the theory. Some levels of the classification appear not to exist for some people, while some rewards appear to fit into more than one category. The most obvious case of this being money, which is certainly useful for fulfilling physiological needs, but can also be seen as a status symbol or as an indicator of personal worth. As to the relationship between the different levels, there appears to be considerable individual differences as to what constitutes satisfaction at any particular level. Consequently most psychologists do not accept it as a valid theory. However, this does not mean that the theory is without value. The classification of needs is useful as a framework for considering possible sources of motivation, and it is likely that people's needs are organized on an hierarchical basis. What has to be recognized is that this hierarchy will vary from person to person.

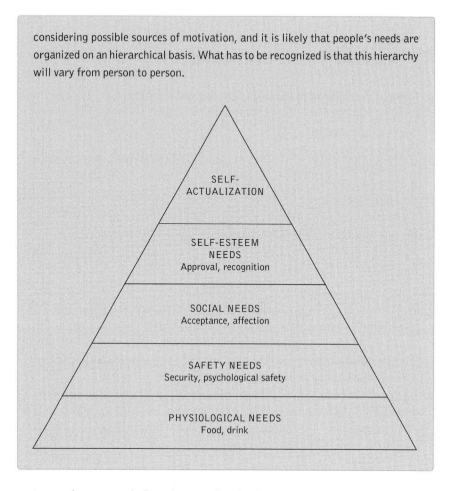

Let us take an example from the area of road safety. Each winter, almost without fail, there will be at least one multiple crash on Britain's motorway system due to drivers driving too close to the vehicle in front in conditions of poor visibility. The newspapers' coverage of the story are almost as predictable as the crashes – 'Motorway Madness' the headlines will scream. The implication is clear: the crashes were caused by people behaving like madmen – an internal characteristic of the individuals concerned. It is unlikely, however, that *those involved* will subscribe to this description. It is far more likely that they will describe their behaviour as being determined by them reacting to the demands of the situation. 'If I leave a large gap between me and the vehicle in front, another driver will pull into it and I'm back driving too close again.' Or 'if I leave a gap in front, the driver behind gets annoyed'. These explanations see the behaviour as being caused by external, rather than internal, factors. The person sees themselves as responding to the demands of the situation, rather than their behaviour being driven by internal factors.

Which of these alternative explanations is correct? It could be argued that the explanations offered by the drivers in the crash are defensive in nature. It is more comfortable to blame external factors, e.g. the situation or other people, than it is to blame oneself. However, there is considerable evidence from social psychology and psychological experiments to show that there are a number of systematic biases that influence our attributions, both for our own behaviour and that of others. One such bias has been hinted at above. It is the *self-serving* bias — we tend to blame others for our failures, and take credit ourselves for our successes. Note, for example, that when the economy is going well the Chancellor of the Exchequer will claim that it is due to his prudent financial management; when it is going badly, the world economy is to blame.

Perhaps the most important bias, however, is in our attribution of the causes of other people's behaviour. There is compelling evidence to show that when doing so, we *over-estimate the influence of internal factors* on behaviour, and *under-estimate the influence of external factors*. When accidents occur, therefore, the evidence suggests that we concentrate too much on the personality and/or attitudes of the 'culprit', and not enough on the external influences on their behaviour. For example, it is well known that there are accident 'black spots' on the roads. If accidents were caused solely by 'bad' drivers, this would mean that all these bad drivers would have their accidents on the same short stretch of road — statistically highly unlikely. (It is perhaps interesting to note, in passing, that this tendency to over-estimate the effect of internal factors varies across cultures. It is most prevalent in the highly 'individualistic' Western countries. It is far less prevalent in the more 'collectivist' cultures of the Far East.)

As well as there being a strong tendency for us to see the behaviour of others as being caused by internal factors, there are other strong pressures that may push us towards accepting such internal explanations. In a managerial context, being able to place the blame on the weaknesses of an individual has its attractions. If the individual is to blame for an accident or some other mishap, such as late delivery or poor product quality, the manager is 'off the hook'. The fear of legal action, either criminal or civil, is largely removed or can be passed on, and the organization need not look too closely at the possible contribution of physical or organizational factors to the accident. Internal explanations, however, are not without problems. If behaviour is caused by such internal factors as 'accident proneness' or 'poor attitudes' there may be considerable difficulties in achieving any changes. Such internal factors are notoriously resistant to such change. For these reasons behavioural approaches concentrate, not on internal factors such as personality and attitudes, but on behaviour. We have tended to concentrate on the attribution of the causes of accidents to illustrate the concept of internal and external attributions and the effect of the self-serving bias because this area provides clear and obvious examples. In addition accident prevention is a significant problem in many organizations. However, the same principles apply other aspects of management. Managers are much more likely to attribute a subordinate's poor performance to lack of ability or to laziness, than to their own possible failure to explain clearly the requirements of the task or provide an effective working environment. This is not to say that internal

19

attributions do not, on occasion, have some validity, but as indicated they are not very useful explanations as it is often difficult, if not impossible, to use them as the basis for effective action.

PERSONALITY

In psychological jargon, such personal characteristics as 'accident proneness' or 'carelessness' are referred to as personality 'traits'. Examples of such traits are too numerous to mention. Almost any description of a person in terms of their personality will involve the use of a trait. Descriptions such as aggressive, outgoing, uncooperative, friendly, etc. are all examples of personality traits. It has been said, not without justification, that the trait is the layman's unit of psychological currency. (It is perhaps worth noting that a description of someone in terms of 'personality' is, in fact, merely a generalization of how they *behave* across a range of situations.) Unfortunately, if we see behaviour as being caused by traits there is little that we can do to change them. A person's personality is very stable over long periods of time and is very resistant to change. Changing a person's personality is something that is likely to require expert help, a long time, and the commitment of the individual concerned.

As we discussed in Chapter 1, describing a problem in terms of the behaviour concerned, rather than personality, brings certain advantages. Unlike personality traits, behaviour may be changed. (We will consider ways of doing this in the next chapter.) Furthermore, what right does an organization have to try to change someone's personality? It is not personality that an organization buys from its employees – it is their behaviour. A job description is written in behavioural terms and the culture and climate of the organization provides the individual with rules and informal instructions about the code of behaviour that is deemed to be acceptable within the company. If the behaviour is appropriate and acceptable then that is all that matters.

The outlook is rather more promising if we see behaviour as determined by 'attitudes', as they are more susceptible to change. However, even the changing of attitudes is not without its problems.

ATTITUDES

There are two main problems associated with trying to influence behaviour by changing attitudes. The first problem is that the relationship between people's attitudes and their behaviour is less than perfect. An example is our reaction to the invasion of privacy of the rich and famous by the media. When public attitudes about such invasions are surveyed the outcome is very clear – between 70 per cent and 80 per cent say they are against such acts. Yet every newspaper editor knows that sales will rise considerably if they print such material! The second problem is that there is considerable evidence to show that the relationship between attitudes and behaviour is more complex than a simple 'attitudes cause behaviour'. Attitudes and behaviour appear to be interrelated. An example of this complex interrelationship can be seen in the wearing of seat-belts in cars. Before the use of seat-belts was made compulsory very few people wore them, despite expensive advertising campaigns. When their use was made compulsory most people complied. It is likely that this has changed people's attitudes to their use. We suspect that, even if the law was repealed tomorrow, most people would continue to wear their seat-belts. (It is worth noting, however, that the advertising campaign may have been necessary in order to prepare people for the change. In some states in the USA a law requiring the wearing of crash helmets for motorbike riders was introduced without a prior advertising campaign to convince those affected of its value. The resistance in those states was so intense that the laws were repealed.)

The relationship between attitudes and behaviour, therefore, is not as simple as might initially be thought and hence we need to examine the subject in a little more detail.

The definition and structure of attitudes

The study of attitudes is one of the most written about topics in social psychology. Questions such as what they are, how they influence behaviour, and how they can be influenced have been the subject of considerable research effort since the 1930s. Originally the term 'attitude' was used to refer to a person's physical posture but it soon came to be used to refer to an internal mental state that is inferred from a person's behaviour. Although there has been considerable disagreement over the years about how attitudes should be defined, most psychologists are now agreed that the fundamental feature of an attitude is that it is an *evaluation*. Eagly and Chaiken (1993) provide the following definition: 'Attitude is the psychological tendency that is expressed by evaluating a particular entity with some degree of favour or disfavour.'

In many respects this definition is very close to that of every-day usage. Attitudes may be held about tangible objects, e.g. football teams, or abstract concepts, e.g. democracy. (It is important not to confuse the psychological concept of attitude with a new use of the term that has being creeping into language from the USA. In this context a person is described as 'having attitude', normally implying an uncooperative arrogance.) Other people's attitudes are, of course, not directly observable. They can only be inferred from what a person *does* when presented with a stimulus to which they respond. In other words, something stimulates a person's attitude, which then expresses itself in certain ways. These different ways in which the attitude expresses itself have typically been classified by psychologists into cognitive (thought), affective (emotional) and conative (behavioural) responses.

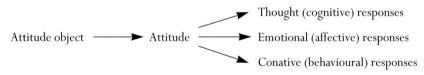

Attitude object ⟶ Attitude ⟶ Thought (cognitive) responses
Emotional (affective) responses
Conative (behavioural) responses

Imagine, for example, the reaction of someone who was suddenly confronted by a large snake. If they showed signs of fear and backed away from the snake, these would be expressions of affective (emotional) and conative (behavioural) responses respectively. In addition, if they were asked what they thought about snakes they might respond that they considered them dangerous, slimy, etc. These would be their cognitive (thought) responses. From these different responses their attitude towards snakes could be inferred. In this case, that their evaluation of snakes was unfavourable. Note that not all of the three classes of responses are present on each occasion. For example you might see the affective and conative responses, but the person may not tell you what their thoughts are about snakes. In addition their thoughts, or beliefs, about snakes may or may not be accurate. For example, snakes are not slimy. Attitudes to safety also follow this pattern. Consider, for example, the reactions of an employee, or group of employees, to the introduction of new working practices. It is often not too difficult to infer their attitudes about the scheme from their cognitive, affective, and conative reactions to it, i.e. what they say, feel and do.

The effects of attitudes on behaviour

Although the definition and structure of attitudes is interesting, the main reason that attitudes are considered important is that they are thought to be a strong, if not the strongest, influence in determining how people behave. Someone with a positive attitude towards, say, safety will, it is assumed, be more likely to behave safely, and more likely to become actively involved in new safety schemes, or someone with a positive attitude to the organization will work harder to achieve organizational objectives. This, however, is an assumption that has, over the years, been called into question.

Perhaps the earliest example of a discrepancy between attitudes and the corresponding behaviour was demonstrated in a study done by Robert LaPiere as long ago as the 1930s. Over a two-year period LaPiere, together with a young Chinese couple, stayed in 66 hotels and other types of accommodation, and ate in 184 restaurants in the USA. At that time there was considerable prejudice against the Chinese, yet on only one occasion were they refused service. Following his experiences, LaPiere sent a questionnaire to all the places they had visited, asking if they were prepared to serve Chinese people. Of the 50 per cent who responded approximately 90 per cent said they would not! This demonstration of an apparent mismatch between attitudes and behaviour has troubled social psychologists ever since. Indeed, it has been repeatedly demonstrated in subsequent studies. A number of explanations have been proposed for this apparent discrepancy. Perhaps the most influential one concerns the level of generality of the attitude. Attitudes are often elicited towards broad categories of entities, for example attitudes towards physical punishment for crime, e.g. corporal or capital punishment. When specific examples arise, however, people's reactions may be somewhat different. The flogging, or execution, of one's fellow countrymen (or, more interestingly, women) in some foreign land often leads to different reactions than might be predicted on the basis of general attitudes towards such punishments. In the LaPiere study, attitudes towards Chinese people *in general* may not predict behaviour towards *these particular* Chinese people at *this particular* time and in *these particular* circumstances.

The effects of behaviour on attitudes

We have considered the effects of attitudes on behaviour, but what of the effects of behaviour on attitudes? It may appear surprising to consider the effects of behaviour on attitudes, as it is normally assumed that the relationship is the other way around. There is, however, considerable evidence to show that, under certain circumstances, behaviour can have a considerable influence on attitudes. There are two main theories that explain this effect, those of *cognitive dissonance*, and *self-perception* theory. For some time it was thought that these theories were in conflict, but recent research has shown that they explain different effects.

COGNITIVE DISSONANCE THEORY

The theory of *cognitive dissonance*, developed by Leon Festinger, has been one of the most influential theories in social psychology. Festinger's fundamental assumption, for which there is considerable evidence, is that people like to see themselves, and be seen by others, as being consistent. This also applies to the relationship between attitudes and behaviour. What interested Festinger, therefore, was the situation in which there was a contradiction between a person's attitudes and the way they behaved. In other words, he was interested in when a person recognized, *cognitively*, that their attitudes and behaviour were in *dissonance* – hence the title of his theory. According to Festinger, a discrepancy between attitudes and behaviour will produce psychological tension. This tension will then produce a psychological drive, the purpose of which will be to reduce, or eliminate, the tension. There are a number of ways in which this may occur.

Consider the situation in which you are being forced to behave in a way that contradicts your attitudes. You may, for example, be faced with the threat of dismissal if you do not behave in a particular way, even though it conflicts with your attitudes. In these circumstances the tension is resolved so quickly that it may not even be experienced. The contradiction can be easily justified – you behaved as you did because you were forced to – you had no option. But what about a situation in which you are influenced, but not forced, to behave in a way that contradicts your attitudes. There is no compulsion – you undertake the behaviour voluntarily. In this situation you cannot resolve the contradiction as easily by invoking the justification of an external, irresistible, force. How then is the tension reduced? This was the type of situation that Festinger investigated.

His original experiments involved university students who were given an extremely boring task to do. At the end of the task it was explained to them that the experiment

23

was to study the effects of people's expectations about a task on their performance and that the experiment required the next group of subjects being told that the task was very interesting. They were then told that, unfortunately, the person whose job it was to give the next group this information had fallen ill. They were then asked if, to help the experimenter, they would undertake this job. Nearly all the students agreed. Festinger had thus created a situation in which there would be a dissonance between attitudes and behaviour. The students would tell their fellow students that the task they were about to undertake was very interesting when, in fact, they thought that it was very boring.

There was another element in the experiment. The students who had been recruited to brief their fellow students were paid to do it. Half of the students were paid $20 (quite a large sum at the time of the experiment), the other half only $1. After they had done the briefing their attitudes as to how boring or interesting the original task had been was assessed. What was interesting was the attitude changes in the two groups. It could be argued that the group that had been paid most would have more favourable attitudes towards the task. In general, the more people are paid the more willing they will be. Thus the highly paid group might be expected to view the boring task more favourably. This, in fact, was not the case. It was the group who had been paid least who saw the task as being most interesting. The theory of cognitive dissonance predicts just this effect! The reason lies in the justification each group can use to explain the difference between their attitudes and behaviour. Consider, first of all, the highly paid group. They can justify the difference between their attitudes and their behaviour as being due to the fact they were being well paid. The low paid group, on the other hand, did not have such a justification available to them. The dissonance could not be resolved by 'blaming' external financial pressures. The only way in which this group could resolve the psychological tension created was by changing their attitudes so as to view the task as more interesting than they originally thought.

The lesson that cognitive dissonance teaches us is seen by some as being counter-intuitive – contrary to common sense. If you want to induce attitude change, get the person to undertake behaviour at variance with their attitude. But in doing so, make as *little* use of external inducements as possible. In this way the person will not be able to justify their behaviour to themselves in terms of the inducements. Their only option is to change their attitudes.

SELF-PERCEPTION THEORY

Proposed by Daryl Bem, self-perception theory takes an alternative, and also perhaps counterintuitive, approach to the nature and change of attitudes. Bem's theory is based on the way that we infer the attitudes of other people. As we have stated above, it is impossible to observe directly someone else's attitudes. Yet we like to feel that we know other people's attitudes, especially those of people we know well. How do we achieve this?

The obvious answer, which was discussed earlier, is that we infer their attitudes from their responses, cognitive, affective and behavioural. Bem takes this process a stage further, and suggests that we infer our own attitudes in much the same way as we infer the attitudes of others – by observing our own responses to the attitude object and then inferring what our attitudes must be! Unlike Festinger, Bem sees attitude change as a system of rational inference, not the result of psychological tensions. These two theories generated much research, often directed at trying to determine which one was correct. Recent studies suggest, however, that both are correct, but that they cover different situations.

It has been known for some time that, for changes caused by cognitive dissonance to take place, the attitude involved had to be important to the person concerned. Often this meant that the attitude concerned had to be important for the person's self-identity. For example, in Festinger's original experiment, most people see honesty as part of their self-identity. Telling lies about the task went against this. This requirement for self-identity to be involved in cognitive dissonance is now recognized as a more general distinction between the two theories. It appears that the important difference is the magnitude of the discrepancy between attitudes and behaviour. Cognitive dissonance works best in those situations where the attitude/behaviour discrepancy is *large*. Self-perception theory, on the other hand, works best when the attitude/behaviour discrepancy is *small*.

TRADITIONAL APPROACHES TO CHANGING BEHAVIOUR

The traditional assumptions about people and their motives, which we have discussed above, have lead to a number of management practices, of varying degrees of effectiveness. As might be expected these have mainly been aimed at changing employee attitudes, something that it is extremely difficult to do, or at enhancing motivation. Interestingly, managers rarely seem to think that it is their own attitudes or motivation that may need to be changed.

Training

Sending people away on training programmes is perhaps one of the most popular ways of trying to improve performance. If the training is to provide, or enhance, basic skills, such as reading balance sheets, operating word processing systems or even the operation of complex machinery or production processes, this can be very effective. But more generic training, such as that designed to improve interpersonal or management skills is much more problematic. One problem with all training is that it is completely ineffective unless the individual(s) concerned really want to be involved. They must want to acquire the skill that is being developed. Training is a cooperative activity requiring the active participation of both the trainer and the trainee. If the trainee does not wish to participate little learning will take place. Despite this, it is surprising how often organizations send people away on training programmes, who either have no idea why they were sent, or who do not want to be there. These two factors may of course be related.

There are many other reasons why training may not be effective – the skills developed may not be relevant to the individual involved; it may be at the wrong level of difficulty; the skill of the trainers may be insufficient. However, even if the training is well designed and implemented, the skills to be developed have been correctly identified, and the trainees are motivated and involved and do, in fact, learn a lot, this may have no effect on organizational performance. This is because the participants are unable to transfer the learning back to their workplace. As will be explained in the next chapter people behave in ways that they find rewarding. Hence they will have found ways that are effective for them in the context of where they work. This context will not have changed while they were away being trained and, hence, despite good intentions, they will rapidly slip back into old behaviour patterns. In general, sending people away on training programmes may be effective for developing specific skills which can be applied in specific situations. It is expensive and generally ineffective at producing more general behaviour change. There are some other techniques, sometimes used, which may be a little more effective

Coaching

It has recently become rather fashionable for managers to employ a coach on a one-to-one basis. This seems to be confined to senior managers and chief executives, possibly because of the expense involved. Coaching is usually aimed at practical issues such as developing future plans, or developing specific skills. It can be very effective since it overcomes many of the disadvantages of training programmes. There is usually a high level of involvement and activities can be tailored to suit the individual. This is a good way of dealing with specific issues for the individual manager, but would be far too expensive, in most cases, to use widely throughout an organization.

Counselling

Counsellors are usually used for dealing with more personal issues, such as helping managers to resolve problems of relationships with their staff or other organization members. The advantages and disadvantages are similar to those for coaching. Both are very dependent on the skill of the coach or the counsellor and on the willingness of the individual to acknowledge possible deficiencies and their willingness to work at improving them.

Mentoring

Many organizations now assign senior and experienced managers to act as mentors to more junior staff. The idea is that the experienced individual will pass on their knowledge and skills and act as a general 'guide, philosopher and friend' to the junior. This sort of arrangement has, of course, been common in organizations on an informal basis for many years. Most successful managers can identify someone, usually fairly early in their career, whom they admired and from whom they learnt much of their skill. Sometimes this is simply from observation. In other cases the senior fairly deliberately developed the other as a sort of protégé. More formal mentoring programmes are intended to place this relationship on an open and more clearly defined basis. Mentoring can be an effective method for developing staff, but depends on the commitment, skill and knowledge of the mentor. A good mentor will provide both coaching and counselling. A poor one will have very little effect. Hence if mentoring is going to be used careful selection and training is needed for those who are going to carry out this role.

Incentive schemes

Many organizations use various sorts of bonus systems to reward good performance. These are based on the superficially sensible idea that if people see that there is a reward for good performance they will be more highly motivated. However, such schemes need to be implemented with care. The issue of the use of rewards is fully discussed in Chapter 3, but briefly, there must be a direct and clear and understood connection between the individual's performance and the bonus payment. Where group bonuses are used, for example, this connection is not clear and they generally have little effect. One of the authors once worked in a company that provided an even more extreme example of this fallacy. All workers were paid a bonus based on the output of the processing plant. As this output depended on the activity of a series of workers who had little contact with each other beyond passing the product on to the next sequence in the process it was quite impossible to tell what effect any individual had on the ultimate level of production. Furthermore, various ancillary workers, such as window cleaners and gardeners, were paid on the same output figures. It is hard to see what effect this was likely to have on their performance. To be fair, this whole bizarre scheme probably owed more to the negotiating skills of the unions involved rather than any coherent management strategy. Another recent and rather strange development is the 'guaranteed' bonuses apparently being built into chief executive packages. It is hard to see what effect this will have on performance and a guaranteed bonus seems to be something of an oxymoron.

Punishing poor performance

The use of punishment is also fully discussed in Chapter 3. Suffice it to say here that it is a very problematic area and is unlikely to be effective. For legal reasons it is also extremely difficult to apply any sort of sanctions in organizations so that it is now rarely if ever used. However, managers do at times show symptoms of wishing that it were possible. Our advice would be not to even think of it.

Getting rid of poor performers

If individuals who are not performing can be removed from the organization this does, at first sight, seem to solve the problem. However, there could again be considerable legal difficulties and costs involved in this approach, all of which is beyond the scope of this book. There is also another factor: the organization has possibly invested considerable time and money in recruiting the individual, there may also have been training costs and investment in salary paid. It seems a pity to lose all this if there is an alternative. It may be possible to devise a strategy to improve performance. That is what the rest of this book is about.

If all the above techniques are so ineffective this raises the question of what do we have that works better. It is the thesis of this book that methods derived from behaviour analysis provide the most effective ways of improving performance and creating behavioural change in organizations. In the next chapter we explain the theory behind this approach and in the chapters which follow show their application in a variety of organizational contexts.

CHAPTER SUMMARY

In this chapter we have examined some common managerial assumptions about what determines people's behaviour. These are, essentially, that behaviour is determined by motivation, personality and attitudes. All three of these are very complex concepts and not very useful for changing behaviour. Motivation is hard to determine and will vary from time to time and individual to individual. Personality is, likewise, hard to determine and to change. Apart from the practical difficulties it would be ethically completely undesirable to attempt personality change in a managerial setting. The relationship between attitudes and behaviour is problematic. While attitudes may influence behaviour, there is also evidence that behaviour influences attitudes. As with the other two concepts attitudes are notoriously hard to change. This led to the conclusion that all the usual attempts to improve performance, such as training, incentive schemes, coaching and counselling are relatively ineffective.

Chapter 3

The behavioural approach to management

In the previous chapter we noted how there is a pervasive tendency for people to attribute the causes of other people's behaviour to 'internal' factors, such as personality and attitudes, and to underestimate the influence that the situation has upon behaviour. But, as we saw in Chapter 1, the problem with this 'layman's view' of the causes of behaviour is that it is not very useful if you are trying to get people to change their behaviour. If behaviour is 'caused' by personality then, in order to change someone's behaviour, you have to change their personality. This is not feasible. Attitudes, on the other hand, are more susceptible to change. As we saw in the last chapter, the problem is that the link between attitudes and behaviour is not strong. Recent studies, for example, suggest that attitudes can only explain between 15 per cent to 20 per cent of people's behaviour.

What are far more important, from a behavioural perspective, are *habits*. Much of our day-to-day behaviour is controlled by habits. This means that we do not have to consciously think about our behaviour – it comes almost automatically. Driving is a common example of behaviour that is largely under the control of habits. These habits have to be learned but, once acquired, we can carry out the required behaviours almost without thinking about them. It is not uncommon, for example, for someone to arrive at work having little recollection of the actual journey. Nevertheless they have arrived without incident. The behaviours of stopping at traffic lights on red, turning at certain landmarks, etc. have been so well learned that they happen almost automatically. They have become habitual.

Habits are, of course, very useful. Having to think about how we are going to behave takes time and effort – thinking is costly. For behaviours that are routine it is highly efficient to have them controlled by habits. As has been mentioned, it appears that attitudes only influence a small part of our behaviour. Research suggests that the situations in which attitudes *do* predict behaviour is when the behaviour is novel. We are then likely to consult our attitudes, to decide how we ought to behave. Repeat behaviours, on the other hand, are likely to become habitual.

At an organizational level it is perhaps worth noting that customer habits are particularly important for organizations that rely on repeat business. Habits that lead people to return to the same record store or supermarket, for example, may be very profitable for the organization concerned. Conversely, the breaking of a previous habit can be costly. The supermarket at which one of us usually shopped was recently closed for some time for refurbishment. During that period a new habit of shopping at a competitor's store became established. When the refurbished store reopened we did not return.

An interesting example of habitual behaviour happened at the authors' place of work some time ago. The fire alarm sounded and, after the normal period of indecision, people evacuated the building in an orderly fashion. What was interesting, to a psychologist, was *how* they behaved during the evacuation. Almost everybody left the building by the way they had entered! This meant that virtually all the occupants passed, or walked away from, perfectly usable, and clearly signed, fire exits. (This meant considerable congestion around the main entrance, with possible safety implications.) Only one small group exited the building using the 'correct', i.e. nearest, fire exit. One of the authors noticed this and asked them why they had used that particular exit. After some questioning it emerged that they had been led out by a relatively new employee who, in her induction training, had been shown which exit to use. Had she not been there it is likely that even fewer people would have used their nearest exit. Habits are, therefore, a very important influence on behaviour and we will now turn to how habits are established and maintained.

Put simply, habits are learned. It is, in fact, an assumption of behaviourism that the vast majority of our behaviours are learned, rather than being instinctive. The debate between those who see behaviour as learned, and those who see it as instinctive, is an interesting one. It also has implications for the 'nature versus nurture' debate. Unfortunately, given the limitations of space, it is not possible for us to do justice to this debate here. Interested readers might refer to Malik (2000).

Assuming that most behaviours are learned can give us some optimism about the possibility of changing inappropriate behaviours. If behaviour is learned it can also be *un*learned, and new, more appropriate, behaviours put in their place. The important question is, therefore, how behaviour is learned.

THEORIES OF LEARNING

There are many theories of learning, but there are two that are most closely related to behaviourism and both use the term 'conditioning', rather than 'learning'. One of these, classical conditioning, we have already covered in Chapter 1. Whilst classical conditioning can give some insight into some emotional reactions and phobias, it is the second form of learning that is perhaps more relevant, and useful, for our purposes. This is known as *operant conditioning* and the name most commonly associated with this form of conditioning is B. F. Skinner (for this reason it is sometimes known as *Skinnerian* conditioning).

Operant conditioning

As we have seen in Chapter 1, in classical conditioning the response is triggered by the stimulus. The hearing of a particular tune causes a feeling of nausea, for example. The behaviour is, therefore, largely under the control of the stimulus that precedes it. Most of our behaviour is, however, not like this. We do not sit passively, waiting for a stimulus to trigger some behaviour. We are active and seek to operate on the environment – hence the term 'operant' conditioning. An important difference between the two types of conditioning, therefore, is that whilst in classical conditioning the behaviour is controlled by stimuli that *precede* it, in operant conditioning the behaviour is influenced by the events that *follow* it. We will now turn our attention to operant conditioning and how it influences our behaviour.

Consequences are at the heart of operant conditioning. Indeed, a single phrase which perhaps encapsulates the central premise of behaviourism is that '*behaviour is a function of its consequences*'. Whether or not a behaviour will be repeated and become habitual or whether it will stop, rarely to appear again, will depend upon the consequences that follow the behaviour. This can be summed up fairly easily in two, apparently obvious, statements.

Only behaviour that is rewarded will continue.

Behaviour that is not rewarded, or is punished, will cease.

Initially these statements may appear so obvious as to be banal, but consideration of them in a little more depth reveals many interesting implications. Let us take the first statement and rephrase it slightly:

If a behaviour is continuing, there must be a reward keeping it going.

(Note that behaviours that are 'one-offs' are not included as they do not fulfil the requirement that the behaviour is continuing.)

This statement applies to all behaviours, but it is not uncommon when we are teaching this material that people will produce examples of behaviours that they believe they continue without any reward, or even continue when they are punished. The theory maintains, however, that such criticisms are not well founded and that there are, indeed, rewards that are maintaining the behaviour. The rewards are, however, sometimes difficult to identify, for two main reasons.

The first, and perhaps less interesting reason, is that rewards are subjective. What one person finds rewarding another may find punishing, and vice versa. Although we are often aware of this, there are times when we fall into the trap of assuming that what we like, others will too. A couple of examples, one from family life, the other from a work context, may help illustrate this point.

Some time ago the secretary one of the authors arrived at work with something obviously on her mind. It transpired that she was having trouble with her teenage daughter. The problem was that of regular, and very heated, arguments between mother and daughter. The behaviour, therefore, was continuing and the author suggested to his secretary that there was, according to the theory, a reward keeping the behaviour going. He also suggested that she was, most probably, the source of the reward. His secretary, not surprisingly, resisted this interpretation. She pointed out that she actually punished the behaviour, by sending her daughter to her room, 'grounding' her, etc. Despite her reservations, however, she agreed to carry out an experiment. Next time her daughter started a row, her mother promised to try not to respond. The experiment worked and, upon questioning, the mother was surprised to find that her daughter admitted to 'enjoying winding her mother up'. This, in the authors' experience, is not unusual in mother–teenage daughter relationships. Fortunately, most daughters seem to grow out of this phase.

Similarly, many young children may have temper tantrums. Tantrums often occur when the child finds that they are not receiving the level of parental attention they desire. In the past they may have received such attention when they were well behaved, but now the level of attention has dropped. In such a situation the child learns, fairly quickly, that if they behave badly they receive lots of attention. It may not be as nice as positive attention, but it is better than nothing! (This pattern of behaviour often occurs when parents are faced with extra demands on their attention – a new child, work stress, a family bereavement, money problems, or a relationship under pressure, for example. Often without realizing it the parents start to pay less attention to the child when they are well behaved, with the result just described.)

The second example concerned a financial services salesperson who spent most of her week 'on the road' in the North of England. Time spent at home was, therefore, precious. Her head office was in Birmingham, approximately 100 miles away, where her boss worked. Her boss, however, did not live in Birmingham and lived during the week in a hotel. As a motivator her boss decided to reward those of his staff who exceeded their sales targets. The reward was to join the boss for a meal in his hotel. The boss was, it appeared, surprised to find that almost none of his sales force achieved the required figures. Most got very close, but few achieved it. The outcome speaks for itself – although the boss thought he was offering a reward it was not perceived as such by most of his staff, who would much rather go home! (In passing, this is a trap that managers should be aware of, and learn to avoid. What managers find rewarding, their staff may not. In psychological terms managers are guilty of a form of 'projection' – projecting their likes and dislikes onto their staff. As Jane Austen wrote in *Emma*, 'One half of the world cannot understand the pleasures of the other'.)

The second reason why rewards may be difficult to find is rather more interesting, and concerns how the rewards are received. This is at the heart of the behavioural theory and it might, therefore, be worth returning to the experimental method of the theory to see the effects in action.

Schedules of reinforcement

Much of the early work carried out by Skinner was on animals, mostly rats and pigeons. (To this day some behavioural psychologists are referred to as 'rat runners' by their colleagues.) Later, experiments moved on to human volunteers and it is said, not without some justification, that the theory is based upon results from 'rats and American undergraduates'.

In order to carry out the experiments Skinner invented a very simple experimental device known to this day as a 'Skinner box'. Essentially it consists of a simple box, into which the animal is placed. The animal, let us say a rat, can move around freely in the box. On one wall of the box is a lever and, as it moves around the box the rat will eventually operate the lever. This lever is linked to a mechanism which, when the lever is pressed, delivers a small reward (normally food) to the rat.

Imagine that you have been placed in such a box (a situation not unlike a novel by Franz Kafka). In the situations that follow we will assume that you have already learnt what the lever does, what we are interested in is how people behave when the lever stops working. In order to be technically correct, we are going to change slightly the terminology we are using. We are going to replace *reward* with the technically correct term *reinforcement*. This is used because the behaviour concerned is being *reinforced*. (For the time being it does not matter if you prefer to think of it as a reward.)

In the first situation you have already learned that every time you press the lever you get a reward. This is an example of what is referred to as *fixed ratio reinforcement* and is normally abbreviated as FR (for fixed ratio). In addition, because pressing the lever is reinforced every time it is referred to as FR1. How would you behave if the mechanism that links the lever to the reinforcer were switched off? It is likely that you would realize fairly quickly that it no longer paid off to press the lever and you would stop doing so. (You might, of course, try pressing the lever after a time, just to see if it had been switched back on.)

Let us now move a situation where pressing the lever paid off after every 40 pushes. This would, of course, be referred to as FR40. Once again you have learned this and, once again, the mechanism is switched off. In this situation you would most probably take about 40 times longer than FR1 to stop pushing the lever but, in psychological terms, this is still fairly quick.

What we have been talking about when we refer to FR1 or FR40 are known in psychological parlance as *schedules of reinforcement*. They specify the rate at which the behaviour is reinforced. But, as well as changing the number of pushes of the lever required we can also change how the reinforcement is delivered. The main alternative to fixed ratio reinforcement is *variable* ratio reinforcement. As an example of the difference between the two let us consider the effects of a reinforcement schedule of VR40 on behaviour.

In variable ratio reinforcement it is as if a randomizer had been placed into the mechanism that links lever and the reward. In a VR40 schedule, for example, the lever-pressing behaviour, rather than being reinforced every 40 pushes, is reinforced *on average* every 40 pushes. This means that it is impossible to predict how many pushes of the mechanism are required before the next reinforcer arrives. It could be the next push, or 40, or 400, or even, occasionally, 4,000 before pressing the lever 'pays off'. If the mechanism were now switched off try to imagine how long it would take you to realize this. We would suggest a very large number of lever pushes indeed.

Examples of variable ratio reinforcement are very common – perhaps the most obvious ones are those associated with gambling, whether it is the national lottery or the stock exchange. For example research has been carried out into a computer-simulated stock market game, using students as subjects. The students were divided into three groups. By controlling the gains and losses they experienced as a result of their investment decisions, each group was reinforced in a different way. The students who experienced a variable ratio reinforcement schedule of returns (gains) at the beginning of the simulation behaved differently from the other groups. In particular they persisted in investing when the stock market began to fall. In fact they actually *increased* the amounts they invested as prices fell even further. After this period of escalation, however, they did finally begin to reduce their investing. The variable ratio reinforcement they had experienced had, however, kept them investing long after the other groups had decided to cut their losses.

This, we hope, demonstrates the power of a variable schedules of reinforcement in keeping behaviour going. It is the most powerful way of maintaining behaviour. This also explains why it is often difficult to find the reinforcer that is keeping a behaviour pattern going. The behaviour only has to be reinforced once every so often for the behaviour to persist.

(It is also worth noting that, as well as ratio reinforcement schedules, there are also *time*-based schedules. For example, the lever will only be reinforced after a certain length of time has passed since the last press that was reinforced. These will not be considered here but they operate in a similar, but usually less powerful, way to ratio schedules.)

Types of consequences

Having demonstrated, we hope, why it is often difficult to identify the reinforcers that are keeping a behaviour going, let us return to the premise that behaviour is a function of its consequences and consider what consequences are possible, and how they might be summarized. These consequences can be that, as the result of behaving in a particular way:

1 we *receive* something *nice*
2 something *nasty* is *taken away*
3 something *nice* is *taken away*
4 we *receive* something *nasty*.

	NICE	NASTY
GIVE	POSITIVE REINFORCEMENT	PUNISHMENT
TAKE AWAY	PUNISHMENT	NEGATIVE REINFORCEMENT

Figure 3.1   *Types of consequences*

They can be summarized quite neatly in Figure 3.1 (adapted from Kazdin, 1994), which also gives the correct behavioural terminology for each.

Let us consider each of these consequences in turn, and let us start by describing the effects of receiving something nice, which we will, from now on, refer to as 'positive reinforcement'. Most people, we find, are fairly happy with positive reinforcement, it is, perhaps, common sense that people will tend to repeat behaviours for which they have received something nice. Negative reinforcement, however, is rather more difficult to understand. So much so that some commonly used textbooks give incorrect descriptions of negative reinforcement and its impact on behaviour.

It is important to realize that reinforcement, *by definition*, leads to behaviour either being maintained or increasing. Reinforcement leads to behaviour being reinforced! Negative reinforcement is no exception to this rule. As we have commented, however, it is not uncommon for psychologists to make mistakes where negative reinforcement is concerned. The difficulty that people experience with the term is most hinges on the word *negative*. We usually associate 'negative' with punishment and, indeed, the most common mistake is to confuse 'take away nasty' in the above diagram with 'give nasty'. A few examples, starting with one from parenthood, will perhaps help in understanding the concept and effects of negative reinforcement.

We find it unpleasant when a baby cries. If, by picking the baby up, we stop it crying, we will pick it up the next time it cries. Stopping the crying negatively reinforces our behaviour of picking the baby up, as it stops the nastiness. (Note that, from the baby's point of view, being picked up is nice and hence the crying is positively reinforced. Next time the baby wants to be picked up, it will cry.) Other familiar examples are fire and

35

burglar alarms. Both of these are based on the principle of negative reinforcement. True, their primary function is to give a warning, but this does not explain why they have to be so loud. The reason for their high volume is that they are designed to drive the occupiers (or, in the case of burglar alarms, the intruder) out of the building. The loud noise is so unpleasant that people move to get away from it. As they get outside the building, the unpleasantness stops. Their escape behaviour has been negatively reinforced. (This is also the principle behind ultra-sonic cat deterrents for gardens.) This is also the reason why it is that it is 'the noisy bearing that gets the oil'. Again, the noise may give some warning as to the state of the bearing, but noisy bearings will often run for a long time. What is more likely is that the noise of the bearing becomes irritating. The oil is applied and the noise stops. The bearing has got its positive reinforcement (metaphorically speaking), and the person who does the oiling is negatively reinforced because the nastiness stops. Because it is important to understand the nature of negative reinforcement we will give a few more examples from everyday life.

At a very basic level eating when hungry is as example of negative reinforcement, as is taking an aspirin when you have a headache. In both cases unpleasant feelings stop as a result of the behaviour. An extreme example of this is the use of certain kinds of torture. 'Tell us what we want to know and the pain will stop.'

Pestering is another good example of negative reinforcement. When someone gives in to someone who is pestering them they reinforce the pestering. The reason why they give in is that their giving in is negatively reinforced – the nastiness of the pestering stops. (Note that pestering is often a very good example of variable ratio reinforcement. We try to avoid responding to the pesterer, but eventually succumb.) A friend of one of the authors, one of Her Majesties Inspectors of Taxes, uses this technique when trying to collect tax debts from bankrupt companies. According to him, other things being equal, the Official Receivers tend to pay off those who shout the loudest. Marketing people are now using the technique of pestering to increase sales to children. Indeed, they refer to it as 'pester power'. The goods are advertised directly at the children, who then pester their parents for the desired goods. Eventually many parents 'give in', thereby stopping the nastiness of the pestering.

We mentioned above that certain kinds of torture use negative reinforcement. For most people the experience that comes closest to torture, we would suggest, is letting double glazing salespeople into your home! Those who have done so often live to regret the decision as it often takes hours to get rid of them. The salespeople are trying to use negative reinforcement to influence the homeowner's behaviour. Their continued presence becomes unpleasant. The only way in which it appears possible to get rid of the salesperson, and hence the unpleasantness, is to sign an order form. The signing behaviour is negatively reinforced – the salesperson leaves. (It is likely that many people will exercise their legal right to cancel the contract following the visit. It is also likely, however, that some will not – another example of the power of variable ratio reinforcement.)

As negative reinforcement works by the removal of something nasty, people very quickly learn to *avoid* the situation that leads to the nastiness in the first place. (For this reason negative reinforcement is sometimes referred to as 'avoidance learning'.) Because of this, although a lot of everyday behaviour is maintained by negative reinforcement, it is often difficult to identify – and to change.

Interesting examples of behaviours that are maintained by negative reinforcement, and which are very resistant to change, are phobias. It is most probably unusual to find work behaviour that is phobic but, for those that are interested, see Box 3.1.

Having considered the two forms of reinforcement shown in the diagram, let us now turn our attention to the two forms of punishment, and their effect on behaviour.

Box 3.1:
NEGATIVE REINFORCEMENT AND PHOBIAS

We have seen how phobias may be 'caused' by classical conditioning. The way they continue to disrupt normal behaviour, however, can be seen as an example of negative reinforcement.

Consider, for example, agoraphobia. The person who suffers from agoraphobia is often unable to set foot outside their house. If they do go outside they experience high levels of anxiety. As a result of this anxiety they retreat inside the house and the anxiety subsides. The behaviour of going back into the house has been negatively reinforced – as a result of behaving in a certain way the nastiness stops.

This explanation also highlights an unfortunate paradox in the behaviour. The problem of the high levels of anxiety experienced outside the house is 'solved' by going back into the house. Unfortunately the 'solution' to the short-term problem of anxiety reduction (going into the house) becomes a problem in its own right – the person is psychologically 'trapped' inside the house.

Another problem that arises with behaviour that is maintained by negative reinforcement is that it is very difficult to change. There are behavioural techniques, discussed in Chapter 1, that can be used but the problem is that people learn to avoid anxiety-provoking situations. To get them to expose themselves to the thing that they fear is often very difficult.

It is perhaps worth noting here that behavioural explanations of phobias do not concern themselves with any 'deeper' explanation for the problem. Other forms of treatment may look to more 'meaningful' past experiences in order to understand and treat the deep 'causes' of the phobia. Proponents of these treatments might argue that behavioural techniques treat only the symptoms, rather than the 'true cause'. Behavioural theory, however, as we saw in Chapter 1, concerns itself only with the external, observable, behaviours. This is, perhaps, both its strength and its weakness.

Punishment can take two forms: the giving of something nice, and the removal of something nasty. Both of these, according to the theory, will lead to the behaviour ceasing, or occurring less often. A good example from everyday life is of imprisonment, which combines both the two forms. It can either be seen as receiving something nasty (the prison environment), or the taking away of something nice (freedom). Unfortunately, however, imprisonment also provides a good example of why punishment is often an ineffective technique for changing behaviour. A very high proportion of those released from prison will be imprisoned again within a few years of their release. Their criminal behaviour has not, apparently, been changed. We will consider the reasons for this shortly.

The effect of both forms of punishment is to reduce the occurrence of behaviour. In the discussion that follows we will concentrate on the 'giving of something nasty', rather than the 'taking away of something nice'. The reason we do so is because the issues involving punishment are clearer for the former. The general rules about punishment as a method of influencing behaviour are, however, the same.

Punishment is the use of an aversive event to change behaviour and, as such, its use is often controversial. For example, debates about the use of corporal punishment, by parents, teachers, or the judicial system are often heated. A distinction needs to be made, however, between 'unconditioned' and 'conditioned' aversive consequences. *Unconditioned* aversive consequences are those, such as physical pain, that are aversive *in their own right*. Anything that inflicts physical pain is an unconditioned aversive consequence. Conditioned aversive consequences, on the other hand, are not inherently aversive – they acquire their aversive properties *by association*. For example, one of the major influences on adult human behaviour are verbal instructions. The instruction 'NO!' from a parent, for example, is usually perceived as punishment by the child, but its utterance is not inherently aversive. If someone were to say the same word in a language that was utterly unknown to you it would be unlikely to be perceived as punishment. (You may, however, realize from their facial expression that something was wrong.)

The use of unconditioned punishment, such as pain, is far more controversial than the use of conditioned punishment, such as verbal admonitions. Occasionally, however, the use of unconditioned aversive consequences may be used as a last resort, but only if it is in the person's best interests. Examples of such uses often come from clinical psychology. For example, minor electric shocks were used on a nine-month-old child who was vomiting up to 100 times a day (see Leslie and O'Reilly, 1999: 284). There was nothing medically wrong with the child, but the vomiting habit threatened to cause serious health problems. As a last resort the child was administered a minor electrical shock to its leg at the start of every instance of vomiting. Over a period of three days the vomiting was entirely eliminated and did not reoccur when the treatment stopped.

Reward/punishment asymmetry

In many cases, such as imprisonment, however, punishment is not effective. In order to consider some of the reasons for the ineffectiveness of punishment we often ask managers to reflect on their own 'criminal' behaviour. Almost all managers will own up to regularly driving above the legal speed limit and occasionally going through traffic lights on 'deep amber'! Both these behaviours are, of course, illegal and can be punished by fines (removal of something nice), or points on the driving licence (getting something nasty), and yet they continue. What *does* stop such behaviours is the presence of traffic cameras that are known to be operative. Most of the time drivers make the quite reasonable assumption that the possibility of them getting caught is very low. The presence of cameras, however, increases the certainty of being caught very considerably. The certainty of being punished has an important influence on behaviour.

This highlights an important difference in the way that punishment and reinforcement operate. Reinforcement, it will be recalled, is best at maintaining behaviour when it occurs on a *variable* schedule. For punishment to be effective, however, it has to occur *every time*. This difference is referred to as *reward/punishment asymmetry*. (Why the term 'reward' is used, rather than the technically correct 'reinforcement', is not entirely clear.)

This is a very important point for anyone who is trying to reduce or eliminate undesirable behaviour. Unless the behaviour can be punished *every time it occurs* the punishment is unlikely to change the behaviour. In most cases, therefore, punishment is not an effective way of trying to change behaviour. We give this advice to managers not because we are 'touchy feely psychologists' who advocate always being nice to people, but for purely pragmatic reasons. As a general rule, punishment doesn't work because it is usually impossible to fulfil the requirement that the behaviour must be punished every time. (Note that, in the case of the child, considered above, the punishment did occur every time.)

A good example of this asymmetry between the effects of reward and punishment was discovered in a factory in which the authors and some of their colleagues were implementing a behavioural safety scheme, which we will describe later in the book. Before starting the intervention the accident records were examined. What immediately stood out was the number of occurrences of minor burns to wrists and forearms – all in one department. Before knowing the exact cause, however, the theory allowed us to predict, in general, what we would find. Since the behaviour was reoccurring, the punishment of the burn could not be happening every time. In addition, since the behaviour continued to occur, there must be a reinforcer keeping it going. The exact cause was later identified. The final stage of a process to make a thin film entailed the film passing, at slow speed, through a heated roller, onto the final take-up roll. Sometimes the film broke. If the operator could catch the film before it disappeared through the heated roller, they saved themselves an hour's work re-threading the machine. Most of the time they did catch it but, just occasionally, the heated roller burned them. Variable ratio reinforcement took precedence over intermittent punishment, as it usually does.

In our experience many accidents follow this pattern. Shortcuts are taken because, most of the time they pay off and rarely lead to punishment. For example, driving too close to the car in front very rarely results in an accident. The reward is, of course, preventing other drivers cutting in and taking the space between you and the car in front.

Some organizations have tried using punishment to influence levels of absenteeism. Following the principle that punishment should occur every time the behaviour occurs, and as soon as possible after its occurrence, those who have been absent are interviewed immediately they return to work. This is usually carried out by the line manager, who decides whether the absence was genuine. If not, the employee is given an informal warning. (Some organizations have implemented this as a requirement for every absence for every employee. In our experience this can generate some ill feeling among managers. Usually managers know their employees and find the 'blanket' requirement inappropriate. Whilst some of their employees may need to be subjected to such a scheme, there are some dedicated employees for who the approach may be counter-productive. The use of such a system should, in our view, be a management skill, to be used at their discretion, not an administrative dictat.)

Although punishment is largely ineffective as a method of changing employees' behaviour, there are, however, other considerations that may have to be taken into account concerning its use – most notably considerations of 'equity'. The workforce may expect punishment of inappropriate behaviour for reasons of 'fairness'. This is acceptable but, when applying punishment for this reason, managers should not be under the illusion that they are likely to have any significant effect upon the wrongdoer's behaviour, except perhaps in the short term.

We have mentioned before that there is often confusion between punishment, (especially the 'giving of nasty') and negative reinforcement. The distinction between them is not easy, and our normal advice to managers writing up behavioural change projects is – 'unless you are *absolutely* sure that you know what the term means, avoid referring to negative reinforcement'. If, however, you are keen to understand the distinction there are some rules for distinguishing between the two.

The most important thing to remember is that, by definition, reinforcement *always* leads to the behaviour increasing. Talking about using negative reinforcement to *stop* behaviour is *wrong*. Also, if the behaviour is decreasing, then negative reinforcement is not operating. The second distinction concerns the timing of the 'nastiness'. Put together, therefore, this produces the following questions:

1 Is the nastiness occurring *before* the behaviour occurs?
2 Does the nastiness *stop* when the behaviour occurs?

Only if the answer to *both* questions is 'yes' is it negative reinforcement.

Extinction

We have now considered the four squares of the diagram shown above, but there is another consequence, which does not fit into the diagram. This is that the behaviour is not rewarded. In other words the behaviour is not punished nor, more importantly, it is not reinforced. If behaviour is not reinforced it will eventually cease – there is no point in doing things that are not, in some way, reinforced. The correct technical term for this is *extinction*, and behaviour that is not rewarded, therefore, will be *extinguished*. If the reinforcer that is keeping an undesirable behaviour going can be identified and removed the behaviour will cease. In fact extinction is a far more effective way of reducing behaviour than is punishment.

Sometimes, however, although the reinforcer can be identified, it may not be possible to remove it. In the case of absenteeism, for example, it is difficult to imagine how the organization could remove the reinforcers that accompany being off work. These, presumably, are those associated with free time for the person to use as they, rather than their employer, chooses. In other situations, however, it may well be possible to remove the reinforcement, especially if that reinforcement is 'attention'.

Before giving a concrete example it is perhaps worth pointing out that *ignoring* is not the same as *non-reward*. The only exception to this is where the *reward is attention*. This mistake is common, even amongst those who have some familiarity with the theory. For example, in a standard organizational behaviour textbook (Huczynski and Buchanan, *Organizational Behaviour*) the following example is given of the use of extinction by a manager trying to influence the behaviour of an employee who consistently hands work in late.

Manager ignores the employee when work is handed in late.

Effect on employee: decreases the undesired behaviour.

It is extremely unlikely that this will have the desired effect, *unless* the employee's main reinforcement is the attention they receive from their manager. It is more likely that the reinforcement for handing work in late is that the employee has a more relaxed time. In addition, if they know that a less liked task is to follow, then spending more time on the current task puts off the less desirable or, if they are lucky, the manager gives the other task to someone else. Ignoring thieves will not lead to a reduction in theft! What *would* lead to a reduction would be if the stolen goods had no value, i.e. they were unusable or unsaleable. Then there would be no reward for stealing the goods. (This, of course, is the principle behind 'coded' radios in cars. The radios are useless without the code – at least in theory.)

A young, unmarried, female manager provided an example where attention *was* the reinforcer. She had recently visited her family in rural Ireland and, during the visit she had met a young man of approximately her own age, with whom she chatted on a number of occasions. On her way back to Dublin airport to fly home, she received a call on her mobile phone from this man. This surprised her, as she had not given him her phone number. (She later found out that he got the number from a family member under a false pretext.) She made it clear to the man that she did not want to maintain contact with him, and that she did not want him to call her again.

Over the next week, however, he tried to call her 23 times, with the number of calls increasing as time went by. She had not answered any of these calls. Her phone displayed the number calling and, when she saw that it was this man calling, she pressed the appropriate button on her phone to terminate the call. She was becoming increasingly worried and rather frightened by this 'harassment'.

Remembering that if a behaviour is continuing it must be being reinforced, she hypothesized that the reinforcement was the act of terminating the call, which meant that the caller was getting a response. She decided, therefore, to remove the reinforcer. She switched off her voice-mail and allowed the phone to 'ring out' whenever he called. The results of doing this are shown in Figure 3.2.

During the first week the number of calls had dropped to 15, and by the second week to seven. By the end of that week the calls stopped altogether and did not resume.

Another example of behaviour that is reinforced by attention is that of nocturnal crying by children who are old enough to sleep through without a feed. (Young babies, of course, may need feeding during the night.) Many parents will have experienced this. The child cries in the night and receives attention and also, perhaps, a feed. Unfortunately this pattern of behaviour may get out of hand, with the child waking more and more frequently during the night. The effects on the parents of the resulting sleep disturbance can be considerable. Eventually the problem has to be addressed. The child has to be left to cry. This will be distressing for the parents, but in the long term is beneficial, for both parents and child. One of the authors has personal knowledge of this with his first child – born before he became a psychologist! The child at that time shared the parents'

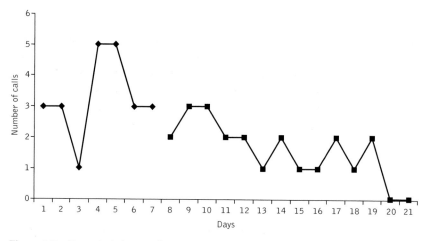

Figure 3.2 *Unwanted phone calls*

42

bedroom in a one-bedroom flat. Eventually the parents had to move out to sleep on the sofa in the lounge and, after checking that the child was not in need, let the crying subside.

One final example may illustrate the effectiveness of the removal of reinforcers. A public nuisance that affects nearly all cities is the defacement of buildings, trains, etc. by graffiti and billposters. Attempts to catch and punish the offenders are largely ineffective, but some organizations have found a way to avoid defacement of their property – by removing the reinforcers! The reinforcement for both billposters and graffiti artists is that many other people see their handiwork. Graffiti artists in particular may feel some pride each time they see their own work on public display. This display often lasts for some time until the owners of the property, or the local authority, gets around to cleaning it off. (In the case of billposters they are often just covered up by later bills.) The solution, therefore, is to remove the offending display *as soon as possible*. This then removes the reinforcers. This was carried out on the building site next to the building in which the authors have their offices. Although there were occasional attempts to deface the eight-foot high hoarding which surrounded the site, they were removed, or painted over, almost immediately (usually the culprits worked during darkness, and the removal occurred soon after sunrise). Very quickly the culprits realized that their efforts were wasted and the hoarding suffered few attempts at defacement thereafter.

There is a phenomenon associated with the use of extinction that perhaps needs mentioning – that of *extinction burst*. It is not uncommon, when a reinforcer is first removed, to find that the behaviour, rather than decreasing, actually increases! This is extinction burst, and research suggests that it occurs in about a quarter of cases where extinction is used. In an attempt to get the reinforcement to start again the person increases the frequency of the behaviour. The effect is, however, relatively temporary. As long as the reinforcement is permanently withheld the frequency of the behaviour will decrease. Beware, however, that the reinforcement does not re-occur – even once. This would be a reintroduction of variable ratio reinforcement. There is considerable danger of this occurring in the example, given above, of nocturnal crying.

There is one final phenomena associated with the use of extinction – aggression. This has been demonstrated in animals. A pigeon whose food reward is stopped will carry out apparently unprovoked attacks on fellow pigeons. In adult humans, however, such overt aggression to fellow workers is, for obvious reasons, rare. What is more common, however, are signs of annoyance. These may take various forms, for example being 'snappy' with others, or slamming doors. As with extinction burst the lesson is to be aware that this phenomenon may happen and realize that it is a perfectly natural part of the process of behavioural change.

Timing of rewards and punishment

Thus far we have simplified situations to look at behaviour that has either positive *or* negative consequences. Much of our behaviour, however, has *both* positive and negative consequences. For example, procrastination avoids the unpleasant task now, but defers it to later. In these situations, which consequence will have the most influence on behaviour, the pleasantness now or the unpleasantness later? The general rule is that *the more immediate the consequence, the more effect it will have*. This applies to both positive and negative consequences.

Let us take two of the possible combinations of timing of rewards and punishment to illustrate the effects.

Let us take a situation where the rewards are immediate but the punishment delayed. Often behaviours that fit into this pattern are those that we know are bad for us in the long term, but nice in the short term. A good example is smoking. Nicotine, it appears, reaches the central nervous system about 2 seconds after inhalation. The positive effects are, therefore, almost instantaneous. In this situation it is the immediate reinforcer that will have the greater effect on behaviour – as any smoker will testify. Another example is 'voluntary' absenteeism. The rewards for taking a day off are immediate, the punishment is often many months away when the personnel monitoring system finally realizes that someone has an unacceptably high level of non-attendance.

The 'opposite' situation is where the punishment is immediate but the reward is delayed. Unfortunately good examples of this type of behaviour are those that are 'good' for us. Taking regular exercise, at the gym perhaps, is good for us in the long run but punishing in the short term. (Unless you are one of those fortunate people who enjoy taking exercise.) Unless we take steps to overcome the immediate punishment it is likely that our good intentions to go to the gym regularly will fade with time. (The 'drop out' rate from gym membership is high and, for this reason, many gyms insist on people signing up for a year.) Once again the more immediate effect (punishment) has a larger influence than the delayed reward (being fit).

The effects of timing also occur in situations of punishment/punishment or reward/reward. An example of the first of these is the wearing of personal protective equipment (PPE), such as ear defenders. Like most PPE, ear defenders are, at least initially, mildly uncomfortable, i.e. punishing. The long-term consequences, such as hearing loss, are also punishing. In this situation, however, the immediate punishment has the most impact on behaviour – that is that PPE is unlikely to be worn.

An example of reward/reward may also be found in the area of safety. It is not uncommon to find that shop-floor employees believe that, when it comes to the crunch, the pressures of production will take precedence in managers' minds over the need for safety. Managers, of course, vehemently deny this. The pressures of the situation are, however, against them. The rewards for achieving production are usually far more immediate than those for having a good safety record. The more immediate reward for productivity will tend to have the largest influence.

The national lottery provides some interesting examples of the power of the timing of consequences. Scratch cards, for example, show the power of immediate, rather than delayed, reinforcement. Whilst the national lottery draw is only twice a week, the feedback from 'scratch cards' is immediate. The evidence is that people become more 'addicted' to scratch cards than the twice weekly draw. (This behaviour is further influenced by the fact that 35–40 per cent of non-winning scratch cards have 'near misses' that also act as a reinforcer.) For the draw itself it is also interesting to note that, according to the lottery operators, half of lottery tickets are bought in the last three hours before the draw, as the potential reinforcement becomes more immediate. (As mentioned previously, the anxiety will also increase if the ticket is not bought. This combination of negative reinforcement and possible positive reinforcement is hard to resist.)

Approach/avoidance behaviour

There is one final phenomenon associated with the timing of consequences that has some interesting implications. This is *approach / avoidance* behaviour. The graphs we will use to describe the behaviour are derived from attaching little harnesses to rats to see how hard they will pull! If this seems somewhat removed from managerial behaviour please bear with us whilst we describe it. We believe it demonstrates an important principle.

In the graphs shown in Figure 3.3 the vertical dotted lines on the right represents the point at which a consequence is received. The horizontal axis represents how far away

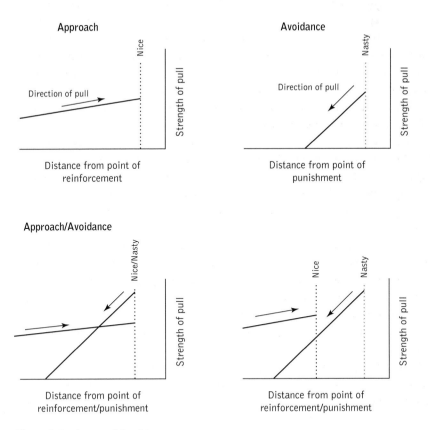

Figure 3.3 *Approach/avoidance*

the rat is from the consequence. In the first graph the consequence is positive, normally food. The rat, therefore, will move towards the food and the line on the graph shows how hard the rat is pulling in order to reach the food. As can be seen, the strength of pull increases the closer the rat gets to the food. The closer you get, the nicer it looks! This represents the *approach* strength.

The second graph, on the other hand, demonstrates how hard the rat will pull to get away from something nasty. Not surprisingly when the rat is close to the nastiness it pulls hard to get away. The further away it gets, however, the less it is inclined to pull. This is the strength of the *avoidance* pull.

Although both graphs slope from right to left it is evident that the graph depicting the pulling away from something nasty (avoidance) is shorter and steeper than that for pulling towards something nice (approach). It is when the two are combined that interesting effects emerge.

(At this point it is worth pointing out that, whilst for rats, it is the physical distance from the consequence which is important, for human beings this can also be time before the consequence is experienced. Unlike rats we have the ability to imagine the future. The horizontal axis of the graph represents, for humans, both distance and time.)

In the next graph the two graphs are overlaid so as to demonstrate *approach/avoidance*. A good example was experienced by one of the authors when he recently bought a new car. Getting a new car is, for most people, nice. Unfortunately, however, it also has to be paid for, which is nasty. The author's pattern of behaviour showed approach/avoidance in operation.

When the purchase of the new car is some time ahead it is the positives that are in the ascendancy. The strength of the approach far exceeds that of the avoidance. As the time of purchase gets closer, however, the strength of the avoidance starts to climb quite steeply until it equals, and then starts to exceed, that of the approach. This is the point of ambivalence and indecision. Any closer to the goal and the avoidance is in the ascendancy, any further away and approach takes over! Hence the indecision.

It is at this point that a good salesperson will step in to try to 'close the deal'. One way in which the decision can be influenced is to move the nastiness far enough away so that the approach is stronger at the time of purchase. This is shown in the final graph. The approach is stronger at the point at which the decision to buy is made. Although the salesperson may not realize the theory behind what they are doing, this is what they are doing when they offer the option of 'buy now, pay later'! Sales managers who have attended our courses have confirmed that this is indeed the case. The 'interest free' or 'pay later' option is, they say, best given at the point of indecision, so as to tip the scales in favour of the 'approach'.

There is another piece of useful advice that flows from approach/avoidance, concerning requesting, and also resisting, favours from others. When a favour is asked it normally involves some extra work, which is considered 'nasty'. Agreeing to do the favour, however, usually leads to immediate thanks from the person requesting the favour. The advice is, therefore, if you are going to ask someone to do you a favour, ask them as far in advance as you can. The immediate reward and the delayed punishment means they are more likely to agree to the request. Who amongst us has not agreed to doing something in the future which, when it is upon us, we regret?

The way to resist the approach/avoidance trap inherent in such requests is fairly simple – it is to bring the punishment closer. When someone asks you to do them a favour, imagine that they are asking you to do it tomorrow, rather than some time in the future.

Earlier in this chapter we made the point that, in operant conditioning, the main influence on behaviour is the consequences that follow the behaviour. This does not mean, however, that consequences are the only influence on behaviour. Behaviour can also be influenced by 'cues' in the environment. In particular, behaviours that have become habits are strongly influenced by such cues in the environment. It is the effect of these cues that we will now consider.

So far we have being considering what maintains behaviour patterns. What also needs to be considered is what initiates the behaviour. As we have seen, much of our behaviour is habitual, and often carried out with a minimum of conscious effort. Habits are, therefore, often very efficient. Complex patterns of behaviour can be executed automatically, allowing attention to focus on the new or unusual.

Obviously, however, the habit needs to take place only when the circumstances are appropriate. Part of the learning of a new behaviour pattern, therefore, involves recognizing the environmental cues that indicate that the new behaviour pattern is appropriate. In behavioural theory these cues are usually referred to as antecedents, as they occur before the behaviour. They are also referred to as *antecedents* so as to make a nice mnemonic *ABC* – antecedents, behaviour, consequences. In our experience, however, the term antecedents is often misunderstood and we prefer the terms *cues* or *triggers*. We will explain why later. Antecedents, therefore, act as a trigger to start the behaviour. It is antecedents which get us going, and consequences which then keep us going.

Discriminant stimuli

As we have seen, the major emphasis in behavioural theory in on the *consequences* that follow behaviour. As well as learning that particular behaviours may lead to reinforcement, however, we also learn the conditions under which the behaviour will lead to reinforcement. The classic example is putting up an umbrella in order to prevent getting wet. We do not put up our umbrellas every time we go outside. We only put it up when we feel drops of rain. The rain is the stimulus that makes us put up the umbrella. For this reason it is known as a *discriminant stimulus*. (The act of putting up the umbrella is then negatively reinforced – the nastiness of getting wet stops.) The technical symbol for this is S^D. Discriminant stimuli are established by differential reinforcement. We learn that if we do something in the presence of a particular stimulus the behaviour will be reinforced. If the stimulus is not present then no reinforcement will be received.

Another example is the telephone. Unless they intend making an outgoing call or to check for messages, people only pick up the phone when it rings. The ring is a discriminant stimulus. (The consequences of picking up the phone will depend upon who is calling, and about what.) Much of our behaviour is under the control of such discriminant stimuli. They indicate when particular behaviours are appropriate (and inappropriate). It is likely that most people's days start with such a stimulus – the alarm clock! Indeed time itself is perhaps one the most pervasive discriminant stimuli. Clocks, watches, and calendars can be seen as mechanisms for producing coordinated discriminant stimuli – time for that meeting, time to go into the lecture, time to catch a plane, etc. Much of our driving is under the control of various discriminant stimuli, in particular road signs. Often our driving to regular destinations is largely controlled by such discriminant stimuli. As mentioned previously, we often arrive at our destination without a conscious recollection of making decisions about the route that we took. Particular landmarks have triggered the turns we have taken to get us to our destination.

Discriminant stimuli are so pervasive that, unless we are aware of them, we may not notice them. Beds are discriminant stimuli for sleeping. In fact, if people suffer from insomnia they are often advised not to lie awake in bed, but to get up. They should then only return to bed when they feel tired and ready for sleep. This is to avoid the bed becoming a stimulus for staying awake, rather than for sleeping. An effective technique for coping with insomnia is given in Box 3.2.

Box 3.2:
STIMULUS CONTROL THERAPY FOR INSOMNIA

Using stimulus control for insomnia is, according to Chesson *et al.* (1999), a 'generally accepted technique with a high degree of clinical certainty'. It works on the premise that insomnia is a conditioned response to time (bedtime), and environmental cues (bed/bedroom) that are usually associated with sleep. The main objective of the technique is to re-associate the cues of time and environment with rapid sleep onset. This is achieved by curtailing sleep-incompatible activities. Thus, if you are suffering from insomnia you should:

a) Go to bed only when sleepy.
b) Use bed and bedroom only for sleep and sex.
c) Get out of bed and go to another room whenever unable to fall asleep (or return to sleep) within 15–20 minutes, and return to bed only when sleepy.
d) Maintain a regular rising time in the morning, regardless of sleep duration during previous night.
e) Avoid daytime napping.

We give similar advice to students who study at home. The environment should be arranged so that there are different stimuli – one for studying and another for relaxing. Ideally the studying should be done in a room other than that used for relaxation. For students this may not be possible, as they often only have one room. In these circumstances they can change the environment by covering their CD player, television set, etc., with a cloth or blanket and perhaps keep a particular chair for study purposes. The stimuli in the environment indicate, therefore, which behaviour pattern is appropriate, making it more likely that this behaviour will occur.

Discriminant stimuli, therefore, have considerable influence over when, and under what conditions, behaviour takes place. As well as influencing people's behaviour by modifying the consequences of behaviour, it is, therefore, also possible to influence it by modifying the stimuli that initiate the behaviour. As we have seen discriminant stimuli are referred to as *antecedents* and, because they initiate it, also as *cues*.

The term 'cue' is perhaps the easiest to understand as it implies that it prompts some behaviour. Actors depend upon for cues from the director or fellow actors so as to know when a response is required from them. (Those who have done any amateur acting will know the problems that can occur if someone gets their lines wrong. This can have the effect of 'throwing' the actors who follow, because the cue they were expecting does not arrive, or arrives in the wrong place.) As with consequences, cues can be used both to stop undesirable behaviour, and to initiate desirable behaviour. Let us look at some examples of each of these.

Stopping behaviour by the *removal* of cues

There are a number of ways in which cues may used in order to stop undesirable behaviour. Once identified the cue may be removed, so as not to initiate the behaviour. One example, from a student's project was to reduce his immediate response to e-mails. This behaviour, he found, interrupted his regular work. The cue that triggered the behaviour was the audible 'ping' produced by his PC when new e-mail arrived. The solution in this case was, therefore, fairly straightforward – turning off the system in the PC that produced the 'ping'.

Yet another student was trying to go jogging regularly. His attempts were proving unsuccessful and he therefore analysed what was occurring so as to prevent him carrying out his plans. When he did so he realized that a major influence on his behaviour were the cues associated with being at home. On arriving home the children would demand his attention and the smell of his wife's cooking would initiate relaxed feelings (another example of a discriminant stimulus). Trying to go jogging after having had a meal and having settled down to relax proved very difficult. His solution was to remove the offending cues by going straight to the jogging track from his last lecture of the day, rather than going home first.

In many situations, however, removing the cue may be impractical. In such cases there are two main alternatives. One is to ignore the cue, in other words consciously override its potential to influence behaviour. This may, however, prove difficult. It is sometimes easier to 'override' the cue. This may be achieved by undertaking a behaviour other than the behaviour that the cue is trying to trigger. For example, a very common behaviour that people often try to stop, with varying degrees of success, is smoking. There are many pharmaceutical products to help the 'sufferer' give up. These include nicotine patches to help cope with the physiological withdrawal effects. What is often more difficult to cope with, however, are the cues that are used to trigger the lighting of a cigarette. One very common such cue is the finishing of a meal. A good example of a way to substitute another behaviour to replace that of lighting a cigarette is that used in some health promotion television commercials. After a meal, do the washing-up! (The commercial also makes the point that it is very difficult to smoke whilst wearing wet rubber gloves!) This latter point is also an example of another possible reaction to cues. Washing-up is an alternative to lighting a cigarette. Wearing wet rubber gloves goes a little further – not only is it an alternative behaviour, but the behaviour is *incompatible* with lighting a cigarette. As we have seen previously, the substitution of incompatible behaviour is a very effective way of coping with undesirable behaviour. If the incompatible behaviour is also the desired behaviour, so much the better. An example of the substitution of behaviour to stop nail biting and picking is shown in Box 3.3.

Box 3.3:
HABIT REVERSAL AND NAIL BITING

Most nervous habits seem to occur when the individual experiences heightened nervous tension. It is thought that habits may serve to reduce the nervous tension experienced by the individual. This reduction in tension would suggest that the habit is maintained by negative reinforcement. Some habits, however, also appear to occur at times of 'boredom', this also might be interpreted as behaviour maintained by negative reinforcement.

Azrin and Nunn (see Martin and Pear, 1996) developed a method called *habit reversal* to treat habit disorders, and research has indicated that habit reversal is an effective treatment for nervous habits, tics and stuttering. Habit reversal techniques have three main categories.

The first category is *awareness training*, in which the client identifies the cues which trigger the behaviour.

The second category is *competing response training*, which involves practising a response that competes with (i.e. is incompatible with) the nervous habit.

The third category is a *motivational strategy*, which includes recording the number of incidents of the habit behaviour.

An example of this, carried out by a number of managers, is the habit of nail biting. Often managers are somewhat embarrassed by the state of their nails and seek to stop the habit.

Although identifying the cues that trigger the behaviour may be useful, the most important element is usually the competing response. An example of such a response might be the grasping one hand with the other for three minutes whenever the subject recognizes or anticipates a nail-biting episode. Other examples might include grasping an object, interlacing fingers, etc. One manager found that the response that worked best for him was to briefly and firmly squeeze or pinch the end of each finger and thumb of both hands in turn. The habitual nail-biter finds pressure on fingernails mildly unpleasant but squeezing them appeared to desensitize them to irritation.

He recorded the incidence of nail biting, both before the intervention, and after. In addition, he also filed his nails smooth as soon as they were long enough, which acted as an additional deterrent to picking. Extra motivation also came from the fact that it was part of a project. The results are shown below. As can be seen the effects were quite dramatic, with the average daily incidence of nail biting falling from 17.4 to 1.65. Towards the end nail biting was effectively stopped.

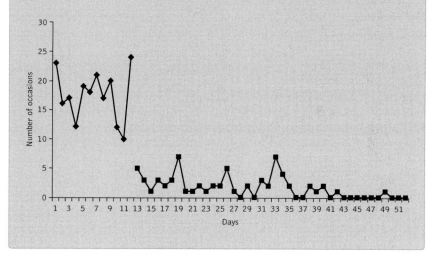

Stopping behaviour by the *introduction* of cues

Two behaviours that society, if not the individuals themselves, wants to reduce is the number of cars that exceed the legal speed limit, and the number that jump traffic lights.

The presence of police officers is likely to be the most effective deterrent to speeding or jumping lights, as the certainty of detection and punishment is very high. It is, of course, not possible for police officers to be there to catch offenders all the time. Perhaps the next best thing, however, are automatic cameras, linked to sensors in the road that detect speeding vehicles, or those jumping lights, and take a photograph of the registration plate. It might be thought that the main purpose of such cameras was to catch as many offenders as possible. If this is so, however, why are such cameras so prominently positioned? Would it not be better to disguise their presence? In fact the presence of the cameras is often advertised. Large signs warning of their presence are often prominently displayed.

The reason for these prominent displays is that the cameras are intended to act as a cue for drivers to reduce their speed. In this they appear to be effective. You only have to watching the brake lights of vehicles as the drivers see the cameras to realize this. The hope is, of course, that drivers will maintain a lower speed for some time after they have slowed down for the camera – they get into the habit of driving more slowly. (What we do not know is if there is evidence as to whether this happens and, if it does, how long the effect lasts.)

This use of cameras for reducing speed illustrates a common feature of cues – they not only indicate when a particular behaviour is appropriate, but when it is *inappropriate*. (Technically a stimulus that *inhibits* a behaviour, rather than initiating it, is denoted S^Δ.) Strange as it may seem, even streets can be designed so as to influence driver behaviour. In a residential area of Manchester streets were redesigned to try to reduce accidents. The pavements (sidewalks) were removed and the surface changed to make it appear more 'pedestrianized'. The street remained a 30 mph zone, but measurements showed that the average speed of vehicles had dropped to $9\frac{1}{2}$ mph.

As with consequences, as well as cues being used to stop behaviour, they can also be used to initiate it.

Initiating behaviour by the introduction of cues

As mentioned above, much of our behaviour is initiated by cues. This is well known by experts on marketing. Organizations often use cues to try to influence us to buy.

On entering a well-known bookshop one winter's day, one of the authors was surprised to find the staff behind the counter wearing coats and sipping hot drinks. He offered to shut the front door, but they replied that it was 'company policy to keep the door open'. It is possible that the reason behind this policy is that people are more likely to enter an open door than one that is closed. Of course, not all people will be influenced by this cue but, given the large number passing the shop-front, it only has to affect a small number of people for it to create more potential customers.

Prompts are now widely used by staff in retail outlets. On being served coffee it is not uncommon for staff to say something like 'would you like something to eat with that?' The prompt may be even more precise. The 'special offer' of the day may be mentioned. The prompts can even be in two stages. When a customer purchases an electrical item the computer linked to the till may well be programmed to prompt the salesperson to prompt the customer by saying 'would you like batteries for that?' Such a prompt is likely to lead to another purchase.

Items that are likely to be bought on impulse are often positioned near checkouts in supermarkets, or the pay-desk in petrol filling stations. The presence of the items, often confectionery, acts as a prompt to purchase. This is exactly the situation with which one of our students had to cope. As she drove long distances for her work she had to fill her car with petrol fairly regularly. This exposed her to the prompts of chocolate. In this situation it is not possible to remove the prompt. She therefore developed a system of rewarding herself for resisting the temptation.

A further example of how cues may be introduced in order to influence behaviour (in this case reduce littering) is shown in Box 3.4.

Box 3.4:
REDUCING LITTER

The organization in this case was an academic institution which had a problem with students depositing litter in communal areas and lecture theatres. (This is, of course, also a problem in many other contexts.) The situation had been highlighted because the cleaning contractor was seeking additional payments for cleaning up the litter. The building concerned was relatively new, but the problem had existed since it was opened three years before. There were around 1,000 students who used the building at various times. There was a cafeteria in the communal area and much of the litter appeared to be associated with this. A large black waste bin was provided in one corner of the communal area.

Many attempts had been made to deal with this problem. Notices had been put on the lecture room doors stating that food and drink were not to be taken into the rooms, but these had little effect. (The situation was not helped by the fact that some academic staff continued to take drinks into the rooms, assuming that the notices did not apply to them.) The Head of Department had also, on occasion, 'read the riot act' to the students, but any effect was short lived.

Analysis

Several issues emerged from the analysis. The attempted solutions were not aimed at the real problem. The problem was litter; but all the messages used in the attempt to control this were directed at trying to stop students taking food and drink into the areas concerned. This was impossible, particularly in the case of drinks. In a long lecture session students were feeling the effects of dehydration from the warm and dry air-conditioned rooms. Furthermore, members of staff were not only ignoring the taking in or consuming of food and drink in the lecture rooms, but were seen to do this themselves, and were thus providing a model for this behaviour. The signs on the doors were not very noticeable. Much of the litter was not food related, but consisted of newspaper and other scrap paper. Litterbins were not clearly available – there was only one large bin in a corner of the communal area and one small one in each lecture theatre.

The solution

As is often the case, the 'traditional' solutions mentioned above had very little effect, so it was decided to try a more behaviourally based approach. This was, in fact, quite simple and depended primarily on the provision of cues. The main cue used was the placing of noticeable litterbins in prominent positions. Signs were placed near the bins. These were of two types, both using coloured graphics, one attempted to appeal to the readers' environmental conscience and the other reminded people to put their litter in the bin. All other notices were removed. Small notices were also placed on the tables in the café area. The effect of these changes was dramatic. In a baseline measure taken over a three-week period prior to the intervention there was an average of 10 pieces of litter on the floor at the end of the day in the communal area and 27 in the main lecture theatre. These were reduced to virtually zero and 16 respectively. Ironically, the litter continuing to appear in the lecture theatre turned out to be mainly surplus copies of lecturers' handouts.

To return, briefly, to the removal of prompts, sometimes prompts are removed when it is desired to reduce consumption, e.g. when the goods are provided free of charge. A large national airline removed such a prompt. On this airline it was customary for a drinks trolley to be wheeled through the cabin, dispensing free drinks to weary businesspeople (and academics returning from a hard day's consultancy work). Although the cabin staff will, if asked, still provide a free drink, the drinks trolley has now been withdrawn. It is the author's perception that, whilst most passengers used to accept a free drink when prompted, few now actually go to the bother of asking. (The 'few' includes, of course, the author who objects to paying ever-higher prices for ever-lower levels of service!) Another case where cues that might be commercially damaging are removed or, more precisely designed out, is in casinos. Casinos want customers to stay as long as possible. In everyday life, however, our behaviour is often strongly influenced by various environmental stimuli, in particular clocks and the amount of daylight. It is rare, therefore, to find a casino that has clocks or windows.

Using cues to teach discrimination

We have seen how cues can be used to start desirable behaviour and to reduce undesirable behaviour. They can also be used together so as to initiate behaviour under some circumstances, but inhibit it under others. One of the authors used this combination of cues to influence the behaviour of a very pleasant, but talkative, student who was beginning to disrupt his working.

The student would typically turn up at the office door and ask if he could 'spare five minutes'. Experience soon showed that, once the student was in the office, it became almost impossible to get him to leave in under an hour. Although the conversations were pleasurable, they were beginning to interfere with the author's work. Talking to managers reveals that this is not an uncommon occurrence in the work-place.

The problem for managers faced with this situation is how to stop the person concerned disrupting their work whilst, at the same time, dealing with the problems the subordinate is raising. (One way to deal with this could be by extinction – not interacting with the person and hence providing no reinforcement. In practical terms, of course, this is not an option that is usually open to managers when dealing with their subordinates.) What are required are cues that indicate to the subordinate when interaction will be reinforced and when it will not. In the case of the student described above cues were used that produced conversations with the student, but allowed the author to control the length of the interaction.

The first cue was used to control the start of the interaction. When the student arrived at the office door asking for 'five minutes' the response was 'not right now, but I could see you at . . .'. If it was convenient, a time was chosen at least ten minutes away. This was done on *every* occasion, so that the student 'learnt' that he would not get immediate attention. (Recall the power of variable ratio reinforcement.) When the student arrived at the pre-arranged time it was suggested that they talk over a cup of coffee in the common-room. (If the person concerned has their own office the manager might arrange to join them there at the chosen time.) This change of venue overcomes the problem of trying to get the student to leave the office. In the common-room once it is decided that the conversation has gone on long enough, the rituals of clearing away the empty cups, plus possible excuses for having to return to the office can be made, bringing the interaction to a natural conclusion.

This simple control of cues means that attention can be given, but in a manner that avoids the disruption to work. The manager now has control over when the interaction starts and how long it lasts.

Some important points about antecedents

There are a couple of final, and very important, points that need to be made.

The first concerns a common mistake that people make when identifying antecedents. Unfortunately there is a difference in the way the word 'antecedent' is used is everyday language and its use in behavioural theory. This difference can lead to problems in undertaking a behavioural change project.

In everyday usage an antecedent is anything that precedes something. So, for example, antecedents are often the history of past events that are thought to have contributed to the current pattern of behaviour. The family problems that an employee has recently experienced are perceived as being antecedents to his reduced performance.

In behavioural terms, however, antecedents are much more precise. In behavioural terms an antecedent is something that not only comes before *but also initiates* (or inhibits) the behaviour. Many events will precede a particular behaviour, but only a few will be the cues that trigger it. For this reason the authors find it more useful to use the term 'cue'. What has to be identified are the *specific cues that trigger the behaviour*.

The other point concerns behaviour that is not occurring. Often the undesirable behaviour is something that is not occurring, but that you would like to occur. For example, you may want to spend at least half-an-hour a day talking to your deputy but, at the moment, this is not happening. When analysing this situation some people are concerned that they cannot find a cue, or antecedent for the behaviour. The simple reason for this is that there will not be one. Cues can trigger a behaviour to start, or stop a behaviour that is ongoing. There cannot, however, be a cue for a behaviour that is not occurring. (There may well, however, be cues that are triggering alternative behaviours and it may well be useful to identify these, so that they may be removed, replaced, or ignored.)

We have now dealt with the 'basic' theory. In subsequent chapters we will show how the theory can be applied to solving people problems. We will also, where appropriate, introduce new material, which will add to the basics covered in this chapter.

CHAPTER SUMMARY

A large part of people's behaviour is habitual and in this chapter we have seen what influences such behaviour both to continue and cease.

The fundamental assumption underlying operant conditioning is that 'behaviour is a function of its consequences'. Whether or not a behaviour will continue or cease will depend upon whether it is reinforced, punished, or extinguished (not rewarded).

Reinforcement, by definition, leads to behaviour continuing and the most powerful type of reinforcement is that which is on a variable schedule. This contrasts with the requirements for punishment to be effective, where punishment must follow every occurrence of an undesirable pattern of behaviour and must be immediate. This is referred to as *reward/punishment asymmetry*.

The timing of consequences will also have an impact on behaviour. Very simply, consequences that occur earlier will have more impact than those that occur later. This is especially important where a behaviour has a number of consequences, some immediate, some delayed.

Finally behaviour can also be influenced by environmental 'cues' (antecedents) which can either trigger or inhibit behaviour. Behaviour can, therefore, be changed by changing these cues.

Chapter 4

Managing yourself and other individuals

It could be argued that all behavioural change involves individuals. We make the distinction, in the chapters that follow, between individuals, groups and organizations on the basis of the main focus of the change strategy. By individual, for example, we mean that the behavioural consequences are specific to an individual, rather than the individual as part of a group or a larger organization.

The approach we will take in this chapter is to use case studies, taken from behavioural projects carried out by students and managers, to illustrate how the theory we have described in the previous chapter can be used to change behaviour. We will also use the cases, where appropriate, to introduce new aspects of the theory.

MANAGING YOURSELF

There are a couple of compelling reasons why it is better to start with describing how behavioural technique can be used to change your own behaviour. First, trying the techniques on yourself is an important learning experience. We cannot, in this book, cover all of the problems you will face when implementing behavioural change. The practical experience of changing an aspect of your own behaviour will make you aware of some of these additional issues.

Second, it is a good rule of management that, if you are going to ask people to do something new, you do it yourself first. Leading by example has its advantages, including reducing possible resistance to change.

In each of the cases that follow there are a number of ways that the problem might be solved using the techniques described in previous chapter. We will concentrate, however, on the actual method used in each case. We will also, where appropriate, explain why the particular method was chosen in preference to other possible solutions.

Case study:
BACK-UP

The client in this case was a manger who was in charge of computer records for a company that had three manufacturing plants, located around the UK. The problem that he had concerned the backing-up of computer files at the end of each working day. There were approximately 20 PCs in each plant and all were linked to the central computer at head office, where the back-up took place. The back-up system was automatic, happening at 9 p.m. each working day, but the automatic back-up system would only work if all the PCs connected to it were shut down. If they were not all shut down the back-up could not take place. The computer system was very reliable and had not yet 'crashed'. The worry was that this reliability had led to complacency. Each PC was the responsibility of a specific operator, but they seemed to have forgotten how important it was that the system was backed-up. Some of them were, therefore, forgetting to switch off their PCs at the end of the working day at 5 p.m.

Those PCs that were not shut down could be identified and reminders about the importance of shutting down were sent out to all those concerned, but the impression was that this had had little effect. Eventually a quick survey was carried out to quantify the extent of the problem. The figures gave cause for concern: in 19 working days the system had only backed-up four times! In one case there were four working days between back-ups. Had the computer crashed at the end of this period almost an entire week's work would have been lost!

At this point it might be worth considering what could be recommended as a solution to this organization's problem.

Possible solutions

One solution that might be considered, bearing in mind the theory presented in the previous chapter, is to think of ways of reinforcing those who correctly shut down their PCs. It might also be worth considering what reinforcers might be used and how these might be given on a variable ratio schedule. It is likely that these would work, but there are some possible problems with using reinforcement in this case. The disadvantages are that the scheme may take some time to set up and to take effect. In fact we have chosen to start with this particular case study because it is one of the few cases where punishment is most probably appropriate.

As we have seen in the previous chapter there are problems with using punishment to try to change behaviour. The two main problems are that, in order for punishment to be effective, it has to occur every time and as soon as possible after the behaviour. Despite this, the use of sanctions to try to influence behaviour is most probably the 'natural reaction' of most people. There is, however, another problem with using punishment – there

59

is often a negative emotional reaction on the part of the punished individual. This may result in some form of retaliation which, in order to avoid detection, is usually covert.

The decision as to whether or not to use punishment has to take into account a number of factors.

1 Can the behaviour be punished every time and immediately?
2 What are the likely costs if the undesirable behaviour continues?
3 What are the likely effects on the individual/s concerned?
4 Is there an issue of equity, e.g. will other employees feel aggrieved if they see unacceptable behaviour go unpunished?

In this case it was possible to identify the individual/s who had not shut down their computers and to deal with them the following morning. Punishment appeared, therefore, to be a practical option. The issue of equity, on the other hand, did not appear to be important. Thus the decision as to whether to use punishment became a cost/benefit analysis involving the benefit of changing the behaviour, and the likely costs of using punishment on those concerned. As the potential costs were considerable and the number of individuals concerned small it was decided, on balance, to use punishment.

The intervention was as follows. At the beginning of each day any computer not shut down was identified. The manager of the individual concerned was then contacted and informed, with the request that they approach the individual as soon as possible and inform them that their behaviour was unacceptable and to explain the possible consequences. During the first four days of the intervention one or two individuals failed to log off. The following day all computers were logged off but the day after that one person did not log off. In the days that followed all the computers were correctly logged off. The problem had been solved in six days.

Because of the requirements for the successful use of punishment, examples of its effective use are not very common. As a general rule of thumb it is much better to try to encourage the desirable behaviour, rather than to punish the undesirable. An interesting example of the effective use of reinforcement in a sporting context is shown in Box 4.1.

Box 4.1:
GOLF PUTTING

The manager concerned had played golf since he was nine years old and had played at international and county level, the latter for over 15 years, off a handicap of one. He had become aware, however, that he was consistently putting short. Research has shown that, for a golfer to consistently hole more putts, the ball has to be travelling at a speed that would take it 17 to 36 inches past the hole.

When he analysed his behaviour he decided that the likely 'cause' of his tentative putting was that such behaviour avoided the possibility of taking three putts. This was also associated with a potential increase in handicap and possible ridicule from fellow competitors.

In order to change his behaviour, and improve his game, he decided to reinforce the desirable behaviour. This behaviour was what he called 'aggressive' putting, i.e. at a speed that would take the ball between 17 and 36 inches past the hole. The reinforcement for this behaviour was provided by his wife, who put money into a savings jar which could be taken out after every third game. The reinforcement schedule was as follows:

Below 6 aggressive putts per 18 holes	Nothing
6 to 10 aggressive putts per 18 holes	£5
11 to 14 aggressive putts per 18 holes	£10
15 to 18 aggressive putts per 18 holes	£20

The number of tentative putts fell from an average of 12.4 during the baseline, to an average of 3.75 during the intervention.

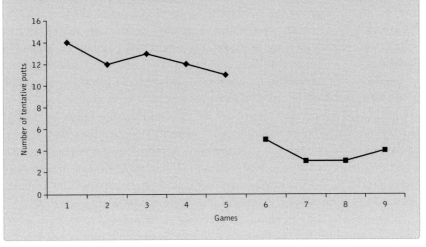

Case study:
SPEEDING

The person concerned was a highly effective sales executive who was in danger of losing her job, not because of her job performance, but because of her driving. Her job involved visiting customers at their premises, all over the North of England. This entailed a large amount of driving and she had just picked up another three penalty points on her licence for speeding. Another speeding conviction in the next three years, therefore, would lead to her facing a possible automatic driving ban. This would obviously create considerable problems both for the person and for her employer.

There appeared to be no discernible pattern to her speeding, as it occurred as much on A and B roads as it did on motorways. She consistently drove at between 20 and 30 mph above the speed limit on motorways, and 10 mph above the limit on other roads.

Solution

In any behavioural change programme the first step is to measure, and record, how frequently the behaviour is occurring before attempts are made to change it. If you do not know how much it is occurring before the behavioural intervention, you will not know whether or not the intervention has been successful. This initial measure is known as the *baseline*. To obtain the baseline level, she recorded her behaviour for a period of three weeks.

In order to get a 'standard' assessment of the scale of the problem she decided to measure the number of times she exceeded the speed limit during a four-hour return trip she made three times a week (a total of 12 hours driving per week). During this period, she recorded, via a Dictaphone, the number of occasions she exceeded the speed limit. Over the three-week period she found the frequency of speeding to be higher than she had expected. On motorways she averaged 16 speeding occasions per journey, and ten occasions per journey on A and B roads. This, she decided, could not be allowed to continue.

The reason why the speeding behaviour continued is relatively straightforward. The immediate consequences of saving time were far stronger than the possible punishment. The punishment was not only delayed, but the certainty of getting caught was also of relatively low. As the punishment could not be brought closer, or made more certain, it was decided to concentrate upon encouraging the desirable behaviour – always staying within the speed limit. She considered using other forms of punishment but thought, most probably correctly, that this would merely have suppressed the behaviour until the study was completed at which point, she thought, the undesirable behaviour would reappear.

At this point, in order to explain the process used, we will need to introduce a new concept – that of the *shaping* of behaviour. Shaping is used when it is unlikely that the desired behaviour will be achieved in one step. This may be the case when the behaviour required is complex, or when to achieve the behavioural goal in one step is unrealistic.

Many behaviours, for example driving a car, are complex and take some time to learn. Others are even more complex, for example learning a language. Learning a language takes years and, given the size of the vocabulary of most languages, it becomes a life-long process. The problem arises as to how the learning of such a complex process can take place. It is said that the infant prodigy, Lord Macaulay, did not utter a word until he was five, when his aunt trod on his foot. When she enquired as to whether or not he was hurt, he made his first utterance – 'thank you madam, the pain has quite abated'! This story is probably apocryphal, but it makes the point about how surprised we would be if this is what normally happened with language skills. Languages are learnt gradually, from birth. The first sound a baby makes is unlikely to be anything like a recognizable word but, eventually, it will make a sound that approximates to a word. Often that word is 'da', which is immediately interpreted by the proud parents as 'daddy' (often to the annoyance of the mother). As soon as it is uttered, the child gets immediate reinforcement, and the sound starts to be repeated more and more frequently. The child has started to learn the language, but we do not normally expect the child to be saying 'da' in the same way when they are, for example, a teenager. We expect them to say 'dad' or 'daddy'. This is achieved by shaping.

When a new, complex, skill is being learned the good teacher will initially reinforce any behaviour that roughly approximates the desired behaviour. Gradually, however, the teacher stops reinforcing the initial, crude, attempts and only reinforces better and better approximations to the desired outcome, thus shaping the behaviour.

The present case presents a nice example of such shaping. The person who was trying to stop themselves speeding decided that, to expect the behaviour to reduce from its present levels (16 occasions per journey on motorways and ten on other roads) to zero in one step was unrealistic. She decided, therefore, to try to achieve the desired goal in three steps.

For first three weeks of the intervention she set herself the goal of driving above the speed limit on motorways on no more than ten occasions per journey, and on A and B roads on no more than six occasions per journey. For the second three-week block the goal was reset to driving above the speed limit on motorways on no more than five occasions per journey, and on A and B roads, no more than three occasions per journey. During the final three weeks the goal was of 'driving on all roads at all times within the speed limits'. Having decided to shape the desired behaviour, the next decision was to decide on what reinforcers could be used to try to encourage the desired behaviour.

The method of reinforcement she used is simple in concept, but a little complicated in practice. She chose a variable ratio reinforcement schedule as this would most probably have greater effect and have more chance of sustaining the behaviour over a period of time. The precise detail of how the reinforcement schedule was made variable is, as suggested, a little complicated. The subjective nature of reinforcement should, however, be recalled. This is the system that worked for her! Bear with us while we describe it.

As she enjoyed solving jigsaw puzzles, she completed a jigsaw puzzle, but left the final three pieces out. She then took a puzzle identical to the one she had all but completed.

From this she took six pieces and added them to the three she had left out of the first puzzle (making sure that the original three pieces were not duplicated). This left her with an incomplete jigsaw puzzle and nine pieces, only three of which would fit the puzzle and complete the picture. She put the nine pieces in a box.

For the first three weeks, if at the end of each day she had achieved her targets, she dipped into the box and drew out one piece of jigsaw. She then tried the piece to see if it would fit into the partially completed puzzle. She repeated this process each day the desired behaviour was achieved until the puzzle was complete.

When the puzzle was completed she then allowed herself to choose an envelope from 20 envelopes, each of which contained a 'treat'. The 'treats' ranged from two tickets to the cinema, dinner for two at a curry house, one-hour beauty treatment, and a new pair of shoes, to dinner for two at a local, exclusive, restaurant. At the start of the second and third three-week periods, she re-assembled the jigsaw and repeated the process until the reward system was stopped after the third three-week period.

We did warn that the method of achieving a variable ratio reinforcement schedule was somewhat complicated, but its effects were very encouraging. Figure 4.1 shows the number of speeding events for each of the stages.

The first set of two lines show the 'baseline', before any attempt was made to change the behaviour. The second two sets of lines show the first two stages of the behaviour change. The third stage is not shown as, by then, the occurrences had dropped to zero. This behaviour was maintained after the reinforcement schedule was stopped. By then the habit had changed. In contacts some months later it was reported that the speeding behaviour had not re-emerged.

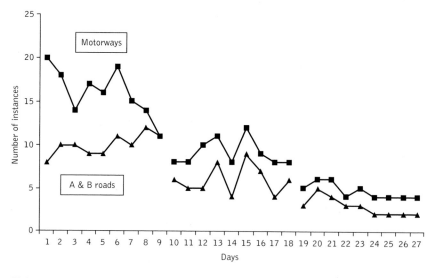

Figure 4.1 *Instances of speeding*

Case study:
SMOKING

Cutting down on smoking is a project chosen by a number of our students. Although it might be argued that it is not directly work-related, there is no doubt that smoking has become an issue in the workplace. Many workplaces are now 'no smoking' and, if only because of the time lost through smoking breaks, it is likely that many employers would prefer their employees not to smoke. Many employees also would like to quit smoking, and may have tried to give up on many occasions.

We will take it for granted that the reasons people continue to smoke, despite the fact that they are aware of the dangers, are self-evident (see section on 'timing of consequences' in the previous chapter).

Solutions

The potential punishments of continued smoking are too far removed to have a major impact on the behaviour. Sometimes 'scare tactics' are used by government advertising campaigns. These often show smokers with will terminal smoking-related illnesses, in the hope that this will bring the potential punishment closer. It is not clear that they are more than marginally effective. As with the previous study, therefore, it may be better to try to encourage the desirable, rather than punish the undesirable.

As with the previous case study, there is an additional concept that needs to be introduced before we consider the procedure used in the present study. That concept that needs introduction is that of the *token economy*.

In the previous chapter we have seen how behaviour can be reinforced. Most commonly, this means that, following the behaviour, something nice is received. We have not, so far, looked in detail at what this might be, other than to point out that rewards are subjective and differ from person to person.

When we considered the way that the behaviour of animals can be reinforced, the main reinforcers used are such things as food and water. These are referred to as *primary reinforcers* – they are the things that are required for life to continue. For animals such as pigeons and rats these are often the only things that can be used as reinforcers, with some degree of certainty that they will be effective. For primates, however, the situation is more complex. Unlike other animals, primates can be taught to undertake behaviours that are reinforced by *tokens*. A major characteristic of tokens is that they have no intrinsic value. What value they have derives from the fact that they can be exchanged for items that do have value. The classic example of a token is money. Bank notes and coins have no *intrinsic* value; they can't, for example, be used as food. Their value is that they can be exchanged for other goods. For this reason money and tokens are referred to as 'generalized reinforcers'. Tokens acquire their ability to reinforce behaviour by their association with the goods for which they can be exchanged, which are reinforcing.

Tokens may then be used as reinforcers which can be 'saved' to exchange for more costly goods. The advantage of a token economy, therefore, is that it allows relatively frequent reinforcement of behaviour, but at an 'affordable' cost. This was what was used in the present case.

The subject had identified that almost all his smoking took place in a pub or bar. Accordingly, as positive reinforcement one token was awarded every time the subject spent more than 90 minutes in a public house or bar without smoking a cigarette. Two tokens could be exchanged for the chance of winning a prize by drawing a ticket from a hat. The hat contained ten pieces of paper, five of which were blank and five of which had a prize written on them. The prizes were:

1 a ticket to a football match of his choice
2 two cinema tickets to watch a film of his choice
3 dinner for two at a local restaurant
4 a complete day off from college work
5 purchasing a compact disc of his choice.

In addition to using reinforcement to try to encourage the desired behaviour, it is often useful to combine this with techniques to reduce the undesirable. When techniques are combined they tend to increase the effectiveness of the intervention. In this case, the manager decided to use both punishment, and the manipulation of cues to try to influence the behaviour.

It was decided that, as a punishment, each time a cigarette was smoked, two pound coins would be thrown into the canal outside the pub where most of his smoking occurred. (It is interesting to note that a common comment to this punishment is 'what a waste, why not give the money to charity?' The problem with this course of action is that giving to charity usually makes people feel good, i.e. it is a reinforcer.)

So as to use all the weapons in the behavioural armoury the subject also identified the cues that initiated smoking a cigarette. These included, for example, seeing a friend light a cigarette. Whenever this occurred he used habit reversal techniques and substituted another behaviour. In this case he would chew a piece of gum.

The combination of reinforcement of desirable behaviour, punishment of undesirable behaviour, and cue manipulation resulted in a considerable drop in cigarette smoking, as Figure 4.2 shows. One year later the manager reports that he still smokes, but far less than previously.

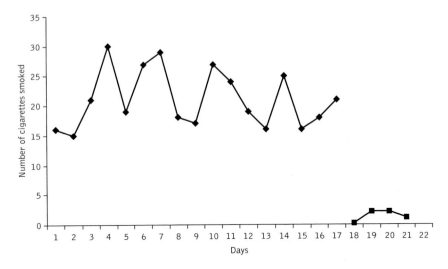

Figure 4.2 *Number of cigarettes smoked*

There is one further additional aspect on the two cases we have just considered that we might usefully note here. That is the use of reinforcement to *reduce*, rather than increase, undesirable behaviour.

The use of reinforcement to reduce behaviour may appear to contradict the theory because, as we have stated elsewhere, reinforcement *by definition* always leads to an increase in the behaviour it follows. As we will see, however, the contradiction is only an apparent one. In the cases we have just considered, those of speeding and smoking, it may appear to an outside observer that the person concerned is rewarding themselves for speeding or smoking, the very behaviours they are trying to stop. What is happening, however, is that what is being reinforced is progressively lower levels of the behaviour. For example the sales agent would reward herself if she hit her target of no more than five occasions of speeding on the motorway. This is known as *differential reinforcement* (DR) and, in this case, the particular form of differential reinforcement being used in that of *low frequency* (L). It is therefore known as DRL.

Another and, most probably, more effective way to reduce undesirable behaviour using reinforcement is by *differential reinforcement of incompatible behaviour* (DRI). In DRI the behaviour that is reinforced is a behaviour that is incompatible with the behaviour that you wish to reduce. Absenteeism is a good example. If a system is used that reinforces attendance this will reduce absenteeism because attendance is incompatible with absence. You cannot do both at the same time.

So far we have been using tangible reinforcers, such as CDs and meals, to influence behaviour. The problem with using such reinforcers is that they cost money. We will now, therefore, look at alternative reinforcers that carry little or no cost.

67

Other reinforcers

Before reading further, try making a list of what reinforcers you have under your control that you can use. Remember that this has to be a tentative list. As we mentioned before, what is a reward for one individual will not be for another. Some people like attending courses. The fun of spending time away from home at company expense tends, in our experience, to fade with familiarity. In psychological jargon, they 'satiate'.

Your list of possible reinforcers will obviously be unique to you. Some managers have control over merit awards and promotion. Most, especially in large organizations, have more limited influence. However, there will be three that should appear on most managers' lists that are very powerful.

Some of the most powerful reinforcers are *social*. Our own self-image can only be sustained, in the long term, if it is accepted by others. Thus, it is to others that we turn for our rewards. This applies even to those individuals who appear impervious to the praise or punishment of others. For them, it is most probably the case that they obtain their rewards from groups outside the organization. In addition we can reward or punish ourselves, but this can not last forever. Such internal rewards need confirmation every so often from other people.

Within the work situation *praise* is used far less effectively than it might be. Variable ratio reinforcement suggests that praise should not be used on every occasion, indeed, if over-used it will eventually lose some of its value. This being said, the evidence is that it is hardly used at all. Why is this? A survey amongst managers suggested a number of reasons. Some took the view that it was inappropriate – their employees were already being well paid for what they did. For the majority, however, it was the embarrassment of giving praise. It is somehow 'not macho'. Many, however, thought that they already did give praise. Over 80 per cent of managers in one organization claimed they praised their employees for work well done. The researchers then asked those employees about the praise. Only 14 per cent said their manager actually gave praise for good work! Another reason for not giving praise is that we tend to 'manage by exception'. We shout and complain when things go wrong (the exception), but fail to praise when things are going routinely well. Compare the number of times you have complained, for example in shops, to the local council, or to other managers, with the number of times you have written complimenting them when they have been particularly helpful.

Praise is a very powerful reinforcer, especially when used on a variable schedule. This schedule should not be indiscriminate or generalized (i.e. the occasional praise for 'work in general'). It should be specific, and very clear to the person which part of their behaviour is being praised. Many organizations are now recognizing that training managers in the appropriate use of praise and recognition has considerable value.

The second powerful reinforcer that all mangers have under their control is that of feedback. Information about how you are doing is a powerful influence on behaviour and yet, like praise, it tends to be under-utilized by managers. The authors have run courses over the years for managers at all levels, up to the main boards of major companies.

With the exception of those at the top a common complaint of managers at all levels is that are not given enough feedback about how they are performing. (We point out to them that, if our experience is to be believed, their subordinates are likely to be saying the same about them.) Even at the most basic level the power of feedback can be demonstrated. Consider computer games, some of which are considered almost addictive. The reinforcer for playing these games is that of trying to improve your own performance, supplemented by almost immediate feedback. This is also the case with many hobbies.

Feedback can also be used to influence behaviour at work. For feedback to be most effective it needs to satisfy the acronym 'PIGS'. Feedback needs to concentrate on the *positive*, rather than the negative. It needs to be as *immediate* as possible and it also helps if it is *graphic*. Finally, as with all behavioural interventions, the behaviour should be as *specific* as possible. An example will show how powerful simple feedback can be in influencing behaviour.

Case study:
SAFETY ON STAIRS

A manager was worried by the number of accidents that were happening on a staircase that led from the office premises to the staff car park. The stairs were metal and not under cover. A number of people had slipped on the stairs, mainly when it was raining and the stairs were wet. Although most of the injuries were minor, a few had resulted in more serious injuries, leading to time off and, in one case, a successful claim for damages. The manager was concerned, not only about the pain and suffering caused to the individuals, but also about the lost time and the possible increase in insurance premiums if the accidents continued. The manager's office overlooked the stairs and he was able to watch how people behaved when entering and leaving the car park. He observed that very few of them held on to the handrail, although there were signs at the top and bottom of the stairs advising them to do so. It was a reasonable assumption that most accidents involved people not holding the handrail, although there was no hard and fast evidence for this.

Solution

The solution to this problem was really very simple and involved giving graphical feedback. Observing from his office the manager simply recorded the number of people behaving safely on the stairs, i.e. holding the handrail. He first established a baseline over a five-day period. As Figure 4.3 shows this was about 35 per cent of those using the stairs. The intervention consisted quite simply of placing a feedback chart at the bottom of the stairs on which was posted the daily percentage of safe behaviour. No other action was taken.

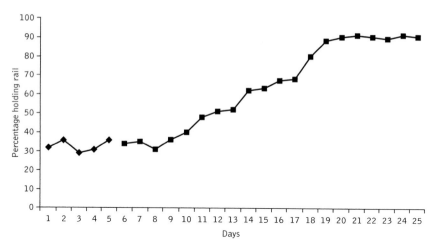

Figure 4.3   *Number holding hand-rail*

As can be seen from the figure, safe behaviour rose to approximately 90 per cent over a twenty-day period.

In Chapter 6 we will see how such simple feedback techniques can have a significant impact on behaviour at the organizational level.

The final reinforcer is less obvious. An American student (Lyons, 1973 quoted in Berthold, 1982), who was working her way through college, made some timings of the average length of time various tasks took in the store where she worked. These timings were averaged across a number of people. Table 4.1 shows two columns of figures indicating the length of time taken to do various tasks in two different situations. As you will see, it took 50 per cent longer to complete the tasks in situation B than in situation A. What reinforcers do you think might have been used to obtain the increase in productivity indicated by the shorter times? Neither praise, money, nor other tangible inducements were involved.

Many of your suggestions might have produced the desired effect, we cannot be sure. It is unlikely that many of you will have found the actual cause. The only difference was that in column A, a nice job was known to be following a nasty job, while in column B a nasty job was known to follow the nice one. To modify Parkinson's law, work expands so as to fill the time available for its completion, but only when the work that follows is nastier!

This phenomenon is known as the 'Premack principle', after David Premack who first observed it in animals. Put generally, more likeable tasks can be used to reinforce less likeable ones. Unfortunately, most of us do not work this way. Rather than do something

Table 4.1 *Time to complete tasks*

Task	Time taken in minutes	
	Condition A	*Condition B*
Stock sweet shelves	20	35
Stock cigarette shelves	5	15
Vacuum floor	5	15
Dump rubbish	5	10
Clean store	45	90
Check in orders	30	60
Aid pharmacist	50	60
Deliver orders	50	60
Total	**210**	**345**

Source: Berthold (1982)

we dislike and then follow it with something we like more, we put off doing those tasks we dislike, finding another task to do in their place. This is known as 'displacement activity', a nice example of which was reported by a survey by the Robert Half Financial Recruitment Agency. When respondents were asked what they did when they first arrived at their office, 34 per cent said they made a cup of tea or coffee, 17 per cent switched on their computer, whilst 12 per cent went to check the post. Only 1 per cent reported that they started work straight away! The Premack principle suggests that starting work straight away would be more efficient. A period of work followed by the reward of a cup of coffee or some other preferred activity will speed up the first work session.

The Premack principle has considerable potentialities as a reinforcer. It is necessary, however, to determine the nature of a person's hierarchy of job preferences if we are to make use of it. There are two main ways of doing this, both of which can be used either on yourself, or on other people.

1 Ask people which tasks they like and which they do not. Usually they will have little difficulty identifying the top and bottom of their hierarchy of preferences. They may have more trouble identifying the relative 'likeability' of tasks in the middle of the hierarchy. This problem can largely be overcome by the second method.
2 Observe and record how long people spend doing various tasks when they have a free choice as to how to allocate their time. The longer they spend on a task, the greater it is liked, and hence the higher up it is in their hierarchy. Given a free choice, people will spend most of their time doing those tasks that they enjoy. (Incidentally, this was the way in which the Premack principle was originally formulated. Animals cannot be asked what they like, but their behaviour can be observed.)

Now we have introduced the concept of the Premack principle, bear this in mind as you consider the following case study.

Case study:
VISIT REPORTS

This problem was raised by a manager of sales agents who make site visits to customers. The problem concerns his agents not submitting call reports in time for a monthly review.

A call report had to be filled in after every site visit. The clear company policy concerning these reports was that they should be dictated into a recorder immediately after the visit and posted in for typing within 24 hours of the visit. This was not happening. Instead, the reports tended to come in all at once, just before they were considered at a monthly meeting of senior management. This created a number of problems for the manager. The typist whose job it was to transfer the reports from the recorders was overwhelmed with reports submitted just before the meeting and some reports were, therefore, not available in time for the meeting. This led to complaints from both the typist and the senior management. In addition the manager suspected that the reports were not dictated until some time after the visit. It might be, therefore, that some useful information was being lost as agents tried to recall what happened during a visit that may have occurred some days before.

The manager concerned also made site visits to the most important customers and he admitted that he was guilty of the same offence as his subordinates! The decision was made, therefore, to start by trying to help the manager change his own behaviour.

Clue It might be worth considering what data the manager might be asked to collect concerning his own behaviour after site visits.

In this case study the manager was advised to monitor his own behaviour when he got back into his car once the site visit was completed. He kept a record of what he did when he got into his car, and the frequency with which he did it. This was then made into a hierarchy, the behaviour done most often at the top and that done least often at the bottom. The results are shown in Figure 4.4. In completing the hierarchy, it became clear to the manager that dictating the report was his *least* preferred task on getting into his car.

The intervention he used to change his own behaviour combined using the Premack principle with changing the cues so as to encourage the desired behaviour.

Using the Premack principle he changed his behaviour so that behaviours higher up the hierarchy could only be undertaken *after* the report had been dictated. These more preferred behaviours became the reward for dictating the report.

Before the change in behaviour was undertaken the manager had noticed that, whilst his mobile phone was easily accessible in the glove compartment, his Dictaphone was normally inside his briefcase, which he placed on the rear seat of his car. In order to encourage immediate dictating of the report he changed the cues. He now ensured that his Dictaphone was kept in the glove compartment, together with spare batteries and tape. His visit report notebook was kept on the passenger seat, and his mobile phone was switched off prior to and during report dictation. In addition, if he had passengers, he told them what he was doing, so that he would not be drawn into his favourite post-visit behaviour of talking to them.

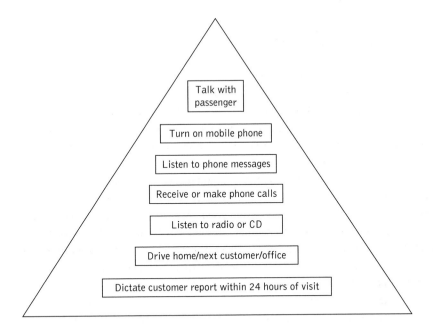

Figure 4.4 *Report-writing hierarchy*

The results of the intervention are shown in Figure 4.5. Colleagues of the manager concerned report that the desirable behaviour is still continuing a year later. The new behaviour has, by now, most probably become a habit.

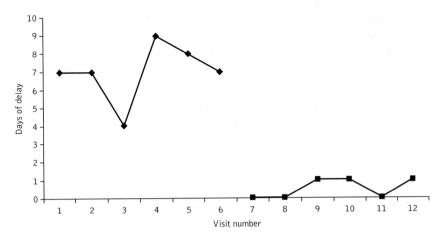

Figure 4.5 *Delay in writing reports*

In our experience the Premack principle is most probably the most useful technique for changing your own behaviour. It is simple to carry out the analysis and to implement. Naturally, if other changes can be incorporated, such as using 'tangible' reinforcers and/or changing the environmental cues, the effects are likely to be even more impressive. Even on its own, however, it remains a simple and powerful technique for improving your own effectiveness.

So far we have considered punishment to stop an undesirable behaviour and positive reinforcement to encourage a desirable behaviour. There are, however, two other consequences that we have yet to consider – negative reinforcement and extinction.

Negative reinforcement is not a technique that can be readily used, especially within organizations, as it requires the imposition of something nasty, which is then taken away when the desired behaviour occurs. For this reason we will not consider it further. (We have only had one project that successfully used negative reinforcement. The person concerned wanted to increase the amount of water she drank. To accomplish this she carried around a 2-litre bottle of water, which was quite heavy. As a result of drinking the water the weight of the bottle diminished.) Extinction, on the other hand, can be successfully used to stop some undesirable behaviours.

Case study:
ADVERSE COMMENTS

A middle manager in a large public utility organization had been sponsored by her employer to do a part-time MBA, which meant that she spent most Fridays at the University Business School. Unfortunately, since starting the course, one of her fellow managers had started making cynical and derogatory comments about her. For example, the manager was not required to be in University one Friday and was in the office instead. On seeing her the manager commented to some of her staff 'What's she doing here on a Friday? I thought she was a part-timer.' Other remarks, although said in a light-hearted manner, were more personal. The fact that these comments were often made in front of her subordinates made them more unacceptable. The manager wished to stop the comments without an argument, as she wanted to maintain her generally good relations with the manager. At the time, these comments were being made, on average, ten times a week.

Solution

When the manager analysed what was keeping the pattern of behaviour going, she realized that she might, inadvertently, be providing reinforcement for her colleague's behaviour. Whenever her colleague made such a remark she responded to it. It might be, she hypothesized, that her response was the reinforcement her colleague was seeking. If it were removed, therefore, the frequency of the remarks should reduce. She therefore decided that, whenever the colleague made such a remark, she would not respond, or would just smile. In the week that she implemented the change the colleague made three such comments on the first day, but thereafter made only one remark during the rest of the week! In fact, by the end of the week he was actually making complimentary comments, which she then reinforced with attention.

Extinction, therefore, can be a useful way of getting undesirable behaviour to cease. Remember, however, the common mistake that people make when using extinction that we referred to in Chapter 3. Extinction is *not* the same as ignoring. If you ignore a thief he will not stop thieving! Extinction requires that the behaviour is not rewarded. Ignoring will not, therefore, lead to behaviour change *except* when the reinforcer is attention.

So far we have looked at how antecedents and consequences can be changed in order to produce desired changes in your own behaviour, in doing so we have drawn on the 'basic' *behaviour modification* (BMod) described in Chapter 3. We will now consider more recent extensions to the theory and what implications these have for improving performance.

COGNITIVE INFLUENCES ON BEHAVIOUR

In the first chapter we looked at two criticisms of behaviourism: the problems associated with trying to explain thinking silently, and emotions. There are others that have implications for self-control, and it is perhaps worth considering these at this point and seeing how the theory has changed in order to cope with these.

The first extension to the theory was *social learning theory* (SLT), a brief description of which may be found in Box 4.2.

As has been mentioned in Chapter 1, behavioural theory is not now the dominant approach to studying psychology. It has been supplanted by the 'cognitive' school, which views human beings as 'information processors'. The most appropriate metaphor for this school of psychology is the human being as a computer and attempts to create 'artificial intelligence' perhaps represent the extreme form of this approach.

More recently SLT has been extended into *social cognitive theory* (SCT) which reflects the important influences that cognitive (i.e. thought processes) play in influencing our behaviour. In particular what we think, especially about ourselves, will influence how we feel, and how we feel will have an important influence on our motivation. How motivated people feel has obvious managerial implications.

Perhaps the most important cognitive concept in SCT is *self-efficacy*. The term was coined by Bandura and his definition of self-efficacy is that it is a set of beliefs about one's

Box 4.2:
SOCIAL LEARNING THEORY (SLT)

Radical behaviourism sees behaviour as being determined by stimuli that initiate it and the consequences that result from it. This presents a largely passive view of the individual. People's behaviour is seen as being determined by factors outside their control. As one poet has put it, 'A creature that moves in predictable grooves, is in fact not a bus but a tram'. This is not how we experience the world. We see ourselves as autonomous beings, capable of making informed decisions about how we behave. Albert Bandura in his *Social Foundations of Thought and Action* pointed out, however, that we do have some personal control over both situations and consequences. Not only does the environment influence our behaviour, we also influence the environment which, in turn, may influence our behaviour. For example, one of the authors will not drive long distances on summer bank holidays. He *chooses* not to do this so as to avoid a highly likely situation (a traffic jam) that will have a predictable effect upon his behaviour (extreme annoyance), which he knows will have adverse consequences (a row with his wife about her map-reading). Although the situation and the consequences may strongly influence our behaviour, we can have a considerable impact on determining both the situation and the likely consequences. This interaction between the environment, the person and their behaviour is known in SLT as *reciprocal determinism*.

Another problem that 'radical' behavioural theory has difficulty explaining is behaviour that occurs in the absence of any obvious consequences. Take, for example, someone starting a new job in a noisy factory. In some factories almost everyone wears ear defenders when appropriate; in other factories this does not happen. What will determine whether or not the new employee wears ear defenders? Radical behaviourism would suggest that whether or not they wear them will depend upon whether or not the behaviour is reinforced. This does not appear to happen. In those factories where ear defender wearing is high new recruits will also wear them, without the behaviour having to be reinforced.

The explanation for this by SLT is that people can learn without having direct experience of reinforcement or punishment. They learn *vicariously*, by watching the behaviour of others. It is sensible when entering a new situation to watch how those familiar with the situation behave and copy them. It is a reasonable assumption that they will be aware of what behaviour is appropriate and what is not. By copying them you are more likely to be reinforced and less likely to receive punishment. New recruits to an organization do not, for example, experiment with their style of dress, or the time at which they leave for home in the evening. They learn what will be reinforced or punished by observing the behaviour of others. In SLT terminology the newcomers are *modelling* the behaviour of others. Some training courses deliberately employ modelling, using either actors or specialists to demonstrate 'good' behaviours that are then copied by the trainees.

The three components, the situation, the behaviour and the consequences, are all capable of being managed. As we have seen, in order to be most effective, behavioural theory suggests that we need to be able to monitor behaviour as closely, and as often, as possible. The person whom we have the ability to monitor most effectively is ourselves. In fact, it could be argued that not only the most effective, but the most economical, form of management is self-management. If we are to manage our own behaviour we need to manage the situation, the behaviour and the consequences in ways that we have already, in some part, considered.

In managing the situation we have seen how cues can initiate or inhibit behaviours. In addition SLT suggests that by choosing our company we can influence our behaviour. Choosing people who will reinforce desirable behaviours will encourage us to change. Also, in order to acquire desirable behaviour it is often useful to choose someone who is skilled and model our behaviour on theirs.

In managing the behaviour we have seen how important it can be to have precise targets or 'mastery criteria'. Criteria for success need to be established that are as precise and unambiguous as possible. It should also be remembered that it may be necessary to 'shape' behaviour. Many complex, skilled, behaviours cannot be learnt in one step; progressive small steps, meeting mastery criteria before progressing, is the rule.

When managing consequences it may often be desirable to eliminate 'extra' reinforcers. Often undesirable behaviour has unintended, extra, reinforcers as well as the obvious reinforcement. Cups of coffee in the common room, as well as being thirst quenching, often have social reinforcers that lead to prolonged breaks. Taking coffee in one's own office does not.

As SLT points out, social reinforcement is important. Using other people as a part of a self-management programme has many benefits. Evidence suggests, for example, that weight reduction classes (which contain many of the elements mentioned here) lead to a reduction in weight. The maintenance of the reduction, however, may often be dependent upon the person's relationship with their spouse or partner.

ability 'to organize and execute courses of action required to attain designated types of performances'. In other words it is an individual's belief that they can behave in ways that will achieve desired outcomes. Such beliefs also have been shown to have beneficial effects. Indeed Bandura originally proposed the concept after noting the better rates of recovery of heart attack patients who believed in their own ability to cope. As well as having positive effects on performance, high self-efficacy also promotes psychological well-being, and helps with stress and depression in threatening situations.

Given the apparent importance of self-efficacy, it is perhaps important to understand what factors encourage it. The sources of self-efficacy lie, to a large extent, in people's past experiences and 'reinforcement history'. It will come as no surprise to find that experience of success, especially if reinforced by social persuasion, is a major source of positive self-efficacy. The successful achievement of goals is an important element in success experiences. This success will, in turn, have an important influence on the goals we then set ourselves. It will also affect how willingly, or otherwise, we accept the goals we are set by others. In self-management, however, we not only have the responsibility for achieving goals but also for deciding what those goals should be.

Self-efficacy, our belief in our ability to achieve our goals, will, therefore, have an influence on the goals we set ourselves. It needs to be remembered that, whilst self-efficacy is influenced by objective events, such as goal attainment, it is, however, essentially subjective. It results from a process of self-persuasion. It is an outcome of our own process of cognitive self-regulation. As such it will be influenced not only by whether we are successful in achieving our goals, but to what we attribute causality for our success or failure. In Chapter 2 we looked at the manner in which people attribute causality for events. The way in which causality is attributed can have significant effects on how we feel and hence our motivation.

We have already discussed the basic distinction made by attribution theory between internal (dispositional) and external (situational) attribution. If we attribute our successes to internal factors, and our failures to external factors (the self-serving bias) our self-efficacy is likely to be enhanced by success and protected after failure. If, on the other hand, we attribute our failures to internal factors, and our successes to external, we are likely to find our feelings of self-efficacy suffering.

The basic distinction, between internal and external causes is, however, rather too simple. We need to add a few more dimensions to increase the power of the theory. Perhaps the best way to do this is to consider what factors are likely to determine performance. For example, to succeed at almost any task we need the necessary basic aptitude, plus we will need to exert effort. In addition, an element of luck may be helpful. In terms of attribution theory both 'aptitude' and 'effort' are internal, i.e. they are personal 'dispositions', something internal to the person. Luck, on the other hand, is normally seen as being external, i.e. part of the situation. (It is interesting to note, however, that some people are called 'lucky' – an internal attribution. For our purposes, however, we will treat it as being external.)

Whilst aptitude and effort are both internal, they differ from one another in an important respect. This is the extent to which they are *stable* or *unstable*. Consider aptitudes such as intelligence or musical aptitude. Such aptitudes tend to be very stable. Like personality traits they do not change very much over time. Whilst there may be techniques to help us make the best use of these aptitudes, there is not a lot that can be done to improve them. The situation with 'effort', on the other hand, is different. The amount of effort we choose to put into different tasks is likely to vary enormously, depending upon, for example, how important the task is, or how much we enjoy it. Whilst aptitudes are very stable, effort is unstable.

Let us now turn to 'luck' and compare it with 'effort'. As we have seen, whilst effort is internal, luck is normally considered external. On the new dimension of 'stability' they are, however, similar. Luck, by its very nature is unstable and transient; it can come and go. There is another dimension of attribution, however, on which they differ – that of 'controllability'. Effort is under our control, luck is not. On this dimension luck is, however similar to aptitudes. We can neither control our aptitudes or our luck.

The importance of these attributions is in their influence over our perceptions of our successes or failures. As we will see, the nature of these attributions will influence how we feel about our performance. This, in turn, will influence what actions we are likely to take in future.

Motivational effects of attribution

Weiner (1985) has suggested that attributions can have a motivational effect. This effect is the result of the emotions generated by our attributions for success or failure. According to Weiner, 'the most embracing presumption . . . is that how we think influences how we feel.' Weiner suggests that the creation of these feelings is the result of a two-stage process.

When faced with success or failure our immediate emotions are automatic, and not dependent upon our attributions for the outcome. Thus success leads automatically to positive emotions, such as happiness. Failure, on the other hand, leads to feelings of sadness. The next stage, however, is unlike the first, as the feelings produced are dependent on the attributions made for success or failure. These feelings are not dependent on specific causes, but the dimensions we attach to those causes, in particular their locus (internal or external), stability and controllability. The emotions aroused then influence the individual's motivation.

For most people, attributions associated with success are easiest to explain. These are normally internal attributions such as ability and/or effort. The first 'primitive' emotion of happiness is followed, therefore, by a feeling of pride. If others were perceived as having helped, feelings may also be of gratitude. Attributions for failure, on the other hand, are rather more complex and, it could be argued, more important in managerial terms.

External attributions for failure are often very useful in that they serve to protect our self-image. For this reason many of us seek an 'external' reason for our failures. If our failure is due to something for which I cannot be held responsible, I am protected from criticism. If we start looking at the causes for our failure using the extra dimensions we have introduced, the picture becomes a little richer and helps explain other possible responses. For example, if the failure is due to factors that, as well as being external are also uncontrollable (task difficulty or luck) then the feelings produced may be those of helplessness (we will return to this shortly). If, on the other hand, the attributions are external and controllable (the actions, or inactions, of someone else) then the likely response is that of frustration and anger, as in 'road rage'. This is usually directed at the perceived cause, for example, the other person. Because of the likely effect on people's self image, however, it is internal attributions for failure that are perhaps more interesting and important.

The most important of these internal attributions are those of effort and ability. If the internal attribution is to a cause that is stable and uncontrollable (e.g. ability), the likely emotional reaction is feelings of shame. Because ability is stable and uncontrollable it cannot be changed. The understandable reaction, therefore, is to withdraw from the situation so that the feelings of shame are not repeated. (Note that withdrawal from the situation leads to the unpleasantness stopping – negative reinforcement.)

Contrast uncontrollable attributions to those where the perceived causes are controllable, for example, the amount of effort put in. If poor performance is seen as due to lack of effort, the likely emotion is that of guilt: you could have succeeded if only you had worked harder. Unlike shame, guilt, at least in Western societies, is a motivating emotion. If performance is due to lack of effort, it can be corrected. The potential is there for increased motivation. (Note that this only applies when the success or failure has some importance to the individual concerned. For most people this will usually be the case.)

The way that people attribute causality, therefore, can have an important influence on their motivation, in particular whether or not they are prepared to persevere in the face of failure. This can have important implications for managers of individuals who may, because of their attributions for failure, be inclined to give up in the face of setbacks.

It is likely that most people will have experienced shame when faced with failure, but this is usually passing and does not have a long-lasting effect. In some situations, however, an 'attributional style' may develop. This may affect some individuals and even, on occasions, whole organizations. This attributional style is called 'learned helplessness'.

Learned helplessness

In its original form the concept of *learned helplessness* (LH) did not include attributional concepts (Seligman, 1975). The attributional elements were added later by Abramson *et al.* (1989).

Seligman was originally testing classical conditioning on dogs. His objective was to condition the dogs to a high pitched tone. To do this he arranged for the dogs to receive a small electric shock to their paws when the tone occurred. (In his book *Learned Optimism*, which can be recommended, he reflects upon the ethics of such experiments.) In this manner the dogs would come to learn that 'tone' meant 'shock imminent'.

The second part of the experiment involved putting the dogs in a 'shuttle box'. A shuttle box is a box with two sections with a dividing partition between them. In one of the sections the floor is metal, allowing mild electric shocks to be delivered to the dogs' paws. The partition is, however, low enough for the dogs to jump over. Not surprisingly, when dogs are given the electric shock they very quickly learn to jump over the partition to escape the shock (negative reinforcement again).

The interesting finding occurred when the dogs who had received the conditioning of 'tone means shock' were placed in the shuttle box. It was expected that these dogs would jump the partition as soon as the tone sounded, without waiting for the expected shock. They did not! Instead they passively stayed in the partition with the metal floor and 'accepted' the shocks. To describe this unexpected phenomenon Seligman coined the term *Learned helplessness*.

Although the original experiments were on dogs, Seligman realized that a similar phenomena can be observed in humans, for possibly the same reasons. Thus LH can be induced by exposing someone to an unpleasant situation where they learn that they can do nothing to remove, or escape from, the unpleasantness. In this situation, once the person realizes that nothing they do has any effect, they give up doing anything at all. Unfortunately, this effect does not remain specific to the original situation. It generalizes to other situations. Thus, in situations where a difference could be made, the person still refrains from doing anything. Some theorists have argued that depressive reactions following trauma can be interpreted as learned helplessness. For example, following the loss of a loved one it is not uncommon to find individuals exhibiting behaviour similar to learned helplessness. Nothing will bring the loved one back, therefore why do anything at all? Like LH this also seems to generalize to other areas of the person's life.

One of the authors has recently observed behaviour that could be interpreted as LH in his own organization. The organization concerned had agreed to merge with another, larger, organization. The 'merger' was to be a merger of equals and the combined organization would have a new name to reflect this. Both organizations were run in a 'quasi-democratic' manner, with committees of staff making the major decisions. Both organizations independently made decisions about, for example, new organizational administrative procedures. These decisions then went to a joint committee, representing both organizations. It soon became apparent, however, that if there was any disagreement, the larger partner's will prevailed, because of its greater voting strength. The reactions of the staff in the smaller organization became ones of resignation and apathy. The view commonly expressed was that there was little point in attending committees, discussing alternatives and recommending courses of action if these were to be routinely overturned.

Although Seligman noted the similarity between LH in dogs and some human behaviours, it also recognized that humans behave differently. When faced with situations that might be thought to induce LH most people, sooner or later, 'bounce back'. It was another psychologist, Lyn Abramson, who suggested that it is not the objective events themselves that produce LH, but how those events are interpreted and, in particular, the attributional dimensions they use. The situations that produce LH will, in general, only produce momentary symptoms of depression, unless they are coupled with a 'depressive explanatory style'.

As well as the dimensions we have already considered (internal/external, controllable/uncontrollable and stable/unstable) there is one more that is involved in the depressive attributional style, that of global versus specific. As might be expected, specific attributions apply to a particular situation only – my tee shot swerved because someone coughed at the wrong moment. Global attributions, on the other hand, apply to almost every situation – my tee shot swerved because I am bad at everything.

All these four dimensions are involved in the self-serving bias we discussed in Chapter 2. When someone fails they will often try to find an 'external' explanation in order to protect their self-image. Not only is the 'cause' of the failure 'external', it is also likely to be due to 'uncontrollable', and 'unstable' factors that are specific to this situation, e.g. bad luck. When they succeed, on the other hand, they tend to attribute it to reasons that are 'internal'. As well as the reason for success being 'internal' it also tends to be 'controllable', 'stable' and 'global'. I can take the credit for my successes because they are caused by, for example, my dedication, motivation and general ability to cope. Thus the explanations for failure and success tend to be mirror images of each other.

In LH, however, the 'normal' self-serving bias pattern is reversed. If I succeed it is because I happened, this once, to be lucky. If I fail, it's because of my inability, as it usually is. The effects of a depressive attribution style are generally deleterious. Pessimistic life insurance agents sell less and drop out sooner. Pessimistic undergraduates get lower grades and pessimistic basketball teams lose more often (Seligman, 2003). Unfortunately LH is often particularly difficult to deal with. The 'depressive attributional style' does not lend itself to change by reasoned arguments (as anyone who has tried to talk someone out of depression will testify). The treatment of such depressive states is beyond the scope of this book, but a milder form of learned helplessness may sometimes be observed in those who have experienced consistent failure at work. (Those who are interested in the treatment of depressions from a behavioural perspective might like to try Seligman's book *Learned Optimism*, mentioned earlier, although the titles given to the attributional dimensions are slightly different.)

The way of coping with such an individual is to take steps to improve their self-efficacy. This involves the setting of mastery criteria that are achievable, providing modelling, etc. In addition, verbal persuasion, when coupled with success, may also have a beneficial effect. Techniques used to combat LH are also commonly used in sports psychology. One such technique, 'attributional retraining', involves training people to avoid 'depressive' style attributions for their failure. Indeed, Försterling (1985) has suggested that such 'retraining' has been consistently successful in increasing persistence and performance.

USING COGNITIVE INFLUENCES TO IMPROVE PERFORMANCE

As we have seen, SCT, whilst recognizing the importance of reinforcement, also places emphasis on thought process and beliefs, especially concerning the 'self'. These beliefs, especially self-efficacy, have an important influence on performance. One of the major ways in which self-efficacy has these effects is through its influence on the goals that people set for future performance. The setting of these goals, and the development of plans for their achievement, plays an important part in self-management. Whilst self-management techniques can be used in order to achieve goals we have been set by others, in many cases self-management involves deciding what these goals shall be.

The setting of goals requires therefore:

- choosing what goals and standards to apply
- preparing a plan of action
- taking action
- evaluating the results of the action.

Choosing goals and standards

We have already discussed the two main influences on the goals that people will self-set. Self-efficacy, our belief in our ability to achieve our goals, will obviously have an influence on the goals we set ourselves, in the same way that it influences other people's goal setting. This will be influenced by the factors we discussed earlier. For example, it is likely to be heavily influenced by our past performances and, in particular, by our attributions for our past success or failure.

Another influence will be the discrepancy between our current performance and our new goals. The size of the perceived discrepancy between these two will have an effect on our motivation. People will tend to set standards that they feel they have a realistic opportunity of achieving. Whilst a moderately sized discrepancy will be motivating, too large a discrepancy will be de-motivating. This will obviously influence, and also be influenced by, self-efficacy.

This self-creation of discrepancies highlights a difference between simple regulating systems and self-regulating systems. Most simple regulating systems, such as a thermostatically controlled heating system, are designed to reduce any discrepancy between the current state and the set standard. People, however, are self-regulating systems and such systems are capable of setting their own standards. This means that they can also change those standards; in doing so they can deliberately introduce discrepancies. For example, even though they have achieved a standard, people will often then set themselves a yet higher standard and try to attain it. We need only watch people playing computer games, or indeed other hobbies, to see examples of this.

Planning

Planning, like choosing, is essentially cognitive. As a consequence, planning and choosing are closely linked and influence each other. For example, our assessments of the success or failure of our plans will influence the goals we set. The planning and choosing stages can be seen as a form of cognitive simulation. Possible behaviours and their likely outcomes and consequences are tried out mentally, before being tried 'for real'. In fact the whole of the cycle described above is tried out mentally and modified as the result of this simulation using mental rehearsal.

There is an aspect of this mental rehearsal that has, until recently, received little attention. This is the mental simulation of the outcomes and consequences of the imagined behaviour. These also form part of the rehearsal, often referred to as mental imagery.

Mental imagery

The use of mental imagery techniques has come into fashion in organizational psychology (e.g. Neck and Manz, 1992). Such techniques have long been advocated by 'popular' authors such as Norman Vincent Peale in books with titles such as *The Power of Positive Thinking* (1990). Until recently, however, such techniques tended to be looked down on by many professional psychologists. One reason for this was the lack of any theoretical basis for such techniques. Developments in cognitive psychology and in clinical psychology have, however, provided theoretical and empirical support for the technique. In practical terms the technique of mental imagery has had most application in clinical psychology. More recently they have been applied, with apparently considerable success, in sports psychology (see Neck and Manz, 1992).

Mental imagery entails the mental creation or recreation of the whole, or part, of an event. This occurs in the absence of the sensory stimulation normally associated with the event in real life. We have already discussed the role of mental imagery in the planning of the behaviour. Possible alternatives can be imagined and strategies tentatively worked out to cope with them. This applies not only to behavioural strategies, but also emotional strategies. This is especially useful where the emotions associated with the behaviour are stressful. For example, speaking in public is considered by many to be stressful. For those who have done it many times, however, the repeated experience leads to a gradual reduction in stress levels. The repeated mental imagining of the behaviour acts in some ways like having the experience itself. Although not as vivid as the actual experience, the mental imaging allows emotions to be anticipated and coping strategies developed. (Recall the treatment of phobias mentioned in Chapter 1.)

There is another function fulfilled by mental imagery that is less obvious. Surprisingly, perhaps, the outcome of an imagined event will influence the individual's level of confidence in their ability to perform successfully. If the event is imagined as having a positive outcome the level of confidence will be higher than if a negative outcome is imagined. Why should this be so, when it is happening only in the imagination?

Human beings are limited capacity information processors. They cannot cope with all the information that is around them. If we are concentrating on one thing, we have, inevitably, to reduce the amount of attention we are paying to other things. In order to cope with this limited capacity people use certain 'short-cuts' when processing information. These normally work well but may, in certain circumstances, lead to 'biases' in our judgements. One of these affects the way we estimate the likelihood of an event occurring.

84

As a general rule, the more frequently we have experienced a particular event, the easier it is to recall. The information processing 'short-cut' that we use when estimating the probability of it happening again is based on this reasonable assumption. This is known as the *availability heuristic*. We judge the probability of an event occurring in the future by the ease with which we can recall it having happened in the past (Tversky and Kahneman, 1974). This method of estimating probabilities usually works quite well. It is, however, subject to other influences which produces the 'bias'. In short, anything that increases the ease with which we can recall an event will lead to an increase in our estimates of the probability of it happening again. For example, one of the factors that can influence probability estimates is extensive media coverage of events. Programmes that report and recreate crimes are likely to increase people's estimates of the probability of crime occurring. An interesting example of this was reported on BBC Radio. The report investigated the growing number of parents in the UK who will not let their children travel to school alone. The reason given by parents was the fear of attacks on their children, in particular fatal attacks. The programme pointed out, however, that the murder rate in children was, in fact, higher in the 1960s than in the 1990s. The number of children murdered by strangers in the UK has remained, according to the programme, relatively stable since 1973, averaging one per year. Many people are also surprised to find that the overall murder rate in the UK is almost the same in the 1990s as it was in the 1930s. This figure is also half of what it was in Victorian times! Yet many people think we live in a more murderous society. Likewise, within the UK the group least at risk of assault is women over the age of 64 whilst the highest is among young men. Interestingly, however, people's perceptions of the risk of being a victim of violent crime are highest in women over 64. These over-estimations may be interpreted as media coverage increasing the ease with which these events can be recalled and hence our estimates of their occurrence. When factors such as level of education and occupation are controlled for, there is a relationship between the amount of crime coverage in the papers people read and their estimates of the probability of such crimes occurring. The more crime reported, the higher the risk estimates.

Ease of recall can also be influenced by imagination. Imagining an event has much the same effect as recalling it. Indeed, the more often an event is imagined the more probable it is judged as likely to occur. For example, people who have a fear of flying often find themselves imagining plane crashes with increasing regularity as the time for their flight approaches. (Any parent who has laid awake waiting for a teenage child to return home in the early hours will have experienced a similar effect.)

We can now see how mental imagery of successfully achieving a performance goal can increase the perceived possibility of it occurring. By repeated mental imagery of success the person's belief in the probability of success is increased. This, in itself, will increase self-confidence and feelings of self-efficacy. This leads to an increased likelihood of success, which itself has a positive effect on self-efficacy. In fact a 'virtuous' (rather than a 'vicious') circle is created.

Mental imagery is one method of cognitive self-regulation. An associated technique is that of positive 'self-talk'.

Self-talk

The most powerful method by which we regulate, or are regulated by, others is through the medium of language. It is the same for self-regulation. Much of our behaviour is influenced by 'internal communications' (Beck, 1976).

The way in which self-talk influences performance is slightly different from the way in which mental imagery has its effect. Both mental imagery and self-talk influence performance by influencing 'thought patterns' (Neck and Manz, 1992). Whilst mental imagery has a direct influence on thought patterns, the effect of self-talk is indirect. To be precise, self-talk, according to Neck and Manz, has its effect by influencing our 'emotional state' which then influences thought patterns. These then influence performance.

The mechanisms by which self-talk has effect are not as well understood as those of mental imagery. However, it is possible to speculate as to how it achieves its effects. One way is likely to be by self-attribution. As we have seen previously, attributions for success or failure have an emotional effect. This emotional effect will then have an effect on our thought patterns. These thoughts are likely to be what is referred to as 'mood congruent'. In other words there is a tendency for thoughts to influenced by, and similar to, the prevailing mood. When we are depressed, thoughts tend to be generally negative. Another likely mechanism by which self-talk influences behaviour is via its influence upon perceived self-efficacy. As Bandura (1986) points out, self-efficacy is a process of 'self-persuasion'. Such self-persuasion often takes the form of an internal dialogue.

However self-talk achieves its effects, there is evidence to suggest that positive self-talk can have an important and beneficial effect on performance. In clinical settings many prominent psychologists advocate its use in treating emotional disorders. As with mental imagery, it is perhaps in sports psychology that the technique is most widely used (see Neck and Manz, 1992).

The methods of self-talk vary slightly, but those suggested by Bandura (1986) are common to many, including Beck (1976).

Positive 'self-talk' involves the following steps:

1 Monitor thoughts. As with the any behavioural change project, the first step is to identify the thoughts concerned, and how often they occur.
2 Pin-point negative talk. Some self-talk will be positive, some negative. The negatives need to be identified and their contents analysed.
3 Stop negative thoughts. Following behavioural principles, behaviour to be discouraged should be punished as soon as it occurs. There are a number of techniques for doing this but one of the most effective is most probably 'thought stopping'. As soon as the negative thought is detected, you should say, out loud

(or under your breath if out loud would be embarrassing) 'STOP!' This has the effect of interrupting the thoughts. At first you may find yourself doing this fairly frequently and loudly. After a time, however, you will find the thoughts occurring less frequently, and you may not even have to verbalize the 'stop'. (This technique is also useful for suppressing recurrent thoughts that may prevent you getting a good night's sleep.)

4   Accentuate the positive. Not only must the negative be consistently punished, but the positive thoughts should be reinforced. You may try to use tangible reinforcers, as discussed in the section on behavioural self-management. It is more likely, however, that your reward will be self-administered praise.

Some examples of self-talk, given by Quick and Quick (1984), are shown in Table 4.2.

Positive self-talk is, in itself, only a tool. You must undertake changing your behaviour if improvements are to be achieved. Behavioural change is quicker than cognitive change. In addition, as will be recalled from Chapter 2, changing behaviour often leads to a change in attitudes.

Having either taken action, or imagined it, the next stage is to evaluate the outcome.

Evaluation

Evaluation involves the comparison of the current state with the self-set standard. The process of evaluation keeps our behaviour in line with those standards. Alternatively, it may lead us to revise those standards.

The emotional and motivational effects of evaluation are most probably best understood in terms of attribution theory (see above). That discussion was, at least implicitly, about standards or goals that had been set by others. There is an additional

Table 4.2   *Positive self-talk*

Situation	Typical mental monologue	Positive self-talk alternative
Difficulty with a superior at work	'I hate that person' 'He makes me feel stupid'	'I don't feel comfortable with him' 'I let myself get on edge when he's around'
	'We'll never get along'	'It will take some effort to get along with him'
Driving to work on a day which you know will be full of appointments and potentially stressful meetings	'Oh boy, what a day this will be!' 'It's going to be hell' 'I'll never get it all done' 'It'll be exhausting'	'This looks like a busy day' 'The day should be very productive' 'I'll get a lot accomplished today' 'I'll earn a good night's rest today'

Source: Quick and Quick, 1984

factor to be taken into account with self-set standards and goals. In talking about standards we have assumed that these are set in a social vacuum, i.e. without reference to other people's standards. This is obviously not the case. The standards of others will naturally have some influence on our own, as will our goal orientation.

Consideration of the evaluation stage brings us full circle, back to the choice, or standard setting, stage. If the standard has not been reached further decisions have to be taken. Further effort may be invested, or standards changed or re-assessed. Self-efficacy may be enhanced or diminished. Alternatively, it may be decided that it is pointless investing further effort into what may be perceived as a hopeless task. Many of these factors will be influenced by the support that the organization provides to encourage effective self-management.

Having considered managing individuals, in the next chapter we will move on to show how these techniques can be used to manage groups of people.

CHAPTER SUMMARY

In this chapter we have seen how behavioural techniques may be used to change the behaviour of yourself and other individuals. We have seen that punishment may sometimes be effective in stopping undesirable behaviour. Unfortunately, it is rare that the conditions required for punishment to be effective (every time and immediate) can be achieved. In general, therefore, it is better to try to encourage the desired behaviour.

Whilst 'tangible' reinforcers, such as token economies, are effective in changing behaviour, there are other reinforcers that are also effective. Social reinforcers and feedback, as well as being effective, are also much less expensive. Evidence suggests that managers consistently underutilize these reinforcers. A potentially very useful reinforcer, especially for use on oneself, is the Premack principle. Tasks that are more liked can be used to reinforce carrying out less-liked tasks.

Finally we have looked at 'cognitive' influences on performance and shown how the attributions that people make for success and, perhaps more importantly, for failure, can influence their motivation. Also of importance is people's 'self-efficacy'; their belief that they can perform as required. The level of self-efficacy can be influenced by both mental imagery and positive self-talk.

Chapter 5

Managing groups

In the previous chapter we demonstrated how a manager can use behavioural techniques to improve the performance of a particular individual. While managers do spend much of their time dealing with people on a one-to-one basis, they are usually also responsible for controlling or improving the performance of groups; normally, the group or department for which they are responsible. Consequently, in this chapter we consider how the behavioural approach can be applied to the management of such groups. We will start, as we have done before, with some examples.

THE UNDER-PERFORMING PROFESSIONAL ENGINEERS

The manager of this department had recently been appointed to this new position in charge of a number of professional engineers, draughtsmen and drawing office staff, who provided a service to a range of other departments. An analysis of the work rate in the preceding twelve months revealed that of the 633 projects received in the department, only 453 had been passed on for action. The remaining 180 were in various stages of completion. The effect of this low completion rate was a continually growing backlog of work, which was causing problems in the organization and considerable dissatisfaction among their customer departments. As a result of this the engineers spent a considerable amount of time hopping from one job to another in an attempt to forestall complaining customers. Consequently, morale was low and the atmosphere was not helped by continual pressure from senior management, who were complaining that the department had the lowest number of completed schemes per staff member in comparison with five other similar departments in the company.

Analysis of the situation revealed no evidence of undermanning – the staff–work ratio was similar to that of other equivalent departments and the engineers were all professionally qualified, some to a very high level, and seemed committed to their work and the organization. However, the number of projects completed by each engineer during the twelve-month period varied considerably, with a range of 40 to 118. The quality of work varied, but in all cases was of an acceptable standard and was often well above the necessary level. It was, however, felt not to be desirable to attempt to lower the standard of work in order to increase output, as this would be likely to be seen as dropping professional standards and would lower morale still further. While the problem was essentially one concerning the output of the department as a whole, we will, for illustrative purposes, concentrate on just two individuals, who are reasonably representative of the group.

Engineer X

The function of the section was to produce designs, which were then passed to the construction section for implementation. Only if unforeseen problems arose was it necessary for the engineer to become involved in discussions with the other section. This could usually be done by telephone; it would very rarely be necessary to visit the site. This engineer, however, was spending considerable time talking to the construction section on the phone and was attending many of the construction site meetings, despite the fact that there was no evidence of any specific problems. This was obviously diverting him from working on other projects. Relationships between the engineer and the construction section were very friendly and it was apparent that the common factor reinforcing both the long telephone conversations and attendance at the site meetings was the social interaction with, and grateful thanks of, the construction section.

Engineer Y

This engineer had a number of roles, in the most crucial of which he was responsible for supplying a highly technical service to all the other engineers. This involved the calculation of complicated settings that were then incorporated, into their schemes, by the other engineers. Premack analysis (see Chapter 4) showed that this particular task was at the bottom of his hierarchy of preferred tasks. His most preferred task was that of 'control engineer'. If the opportunity arose he would volunteer to undertake this task, for which he received the gratitude of those for whom he was 'standing in'. If this option was not available, he would next choose to undertake his function of organizing plant and equipment. This task was repetitive and required little in the way of technical skills. Although there was a clerk available to undertake the more mundane tasks involved, the engineer insisted on completing them himself. At the bottom of his hierarchy was the most important and technically demanding aspect of his job. This was only carried out when all other options had been exhausted or when external pressures from others forced him to undertake them. One reason for the low ranking of this task may well have been the possibility of negative consequences associated with it. The task was technically demanding and hence errors could be made, and the consequences of such errors were potentially serious. There were, therefore, few rewards for undertaking the task and potentially strong punishment for any errors.

The situation was further complicated by the fact that this current section of engineers had recently been created by combining two previously geographically distinct groups.

Until this reorganization Y had been head of one of these groups. At the reorganization the manager of the other group was appointed as the head of the combined section. As a result, Y was perceived by others as having been 'shunted sideways', with consequent loss of status. Before the reorganization he had shown a high work rate and had often worked long hours. Latterly, his work rate was low and he exhibited clear signs of 'clock watching'.

The solution

The approach adopted to improve the performance of the group was essentially the same for each engineer, but with minor variations to take into account any particular significant aspects of an individual's situation. The general procedure followed was based on the three essential steps of the behavioural approach. Namely:

1 specify precisely the desired behaviour
2 reinforce the performance of the desired behaviour
3 remove reinforcement from undesired behaviour.

The ultimate behaviour required was the production of more schemes than were previously being produced. Individual targets were, therefore, set for each of the engineers. The target for each individual was based on the level of work over the previous twelve months and was agreed with the individual concerned. Thus the target levels set for each engineer differed quite widely. Despite this wide variation, the targets set were accepted as generally fair by all those involved. The most likely reason for the general acceptance of these unequal targets was that none of the engineers was perceived, by their colleagues, as not 'pulling their weight', and those with lower targets were contributing to the department's work in other ways.

These targets are essentially 'outcomes' and while some reinforcement of these was legitimate, it was important to identify the behaviours that would lead to these outcomes and find appropriate ways in which to reinforce such behaviours. Potentially, there are many reinforcers that could be used in this context. Unfortunately, many of them, such as paying bonuses or giving time off, cost money and are often not available to individual managers. However, there are two very powerful reinforcers that lie within any manager's control: feedback, and praise and recognition. These were the two used in this case, but in slightly different ways with each engineer, since each case was different. To illustrate with our two engineers X and Y:

Engineer X

Ideally, it would be beneficial to remove the social reinforcement this engineer was receiving from the construction section, which was undoubtedly contributing to keeping his helpful behaviour going. (Helpful to the construction section that is, not to his own group.) However, it is extremely difficult to get others, over whom you may have no

91

control, to stop giving social reinforcement. To stop such social interaction would often be seen as rudeness on the part of the participants and, in any case, the construction section valued his help and would want to keep it going. Accordingly, the strategy adopted was to use reinforcement of the desired behaviour, in the hope it would prove more powerful than the social reinforcement provided by the other section. The precise method used involved frequent meetings with the manager at which progress towards meeting targets would be reviewed and feedback and praise given for achieving improved scheme production.

Engineer Y

The strategy used with this engineer involved one slight difference from that used with the others. As well as reinforcing the desired behaviour it was decided to remove, or at least lessen, the possibility of punishment as a result of incorrect calculations. This was done by providing additional training on this aspect of the job. Once this training had been given, frequent meetings were arranged at which the increased completion rate of the tasks was reinforced. The reinforcement used was the same as that for the other engineers: regular feedback plus praise for improved performance.

The outcome

The results of this intervention were impressive. A year later the performance of all the engineers had improved. The section as a whole went from being the worst performing of the five similar sections in the company to being the top performing one. Comparison of the performance figures for the six months immediately preceding the introduction of the above changes with the equivalent six months a year later showed an increase of 73 per cent.

The above case could be seen as an example of a manager using behavioural techniques with his subordinates on a one-to-one basis, as discussed in the previous chapter. However, it is included here because it did involve the analysis of the behaviour of all members of the group and then the development of a strategy which was applied to the whole section, albeit with slight variations from individual to individual. It was also done with the aim of improving total group performance. The following example describes a more traditional and equally successful intervention, in which significant behaviour change was achieved by the introduction of a standard programme of reinforcement across an entire and large group.

ENCOURAGING THE WEARING OF EAR DEFENDERS

Two researchers, Dov Zohar and Nahum Fussfeld (1981), implemented this behavioural safety scheme in an Israeli textile factory, the objective of which was to increase the use of ear protection in a noisy industrial environment. Despite very high noise levels in the weaving sheds (averaging 106 dBA), only about 30 per cent of workers in those areas were wearing ear defenders, although these were provided by the management and were freely available. Many attempts had been made to increase this figure without much success. These included the usual strategies to change attitudes (management exhortation and posters) and the use of discipline. When asked why the ear defenders were not worn, workers said that they were uncomfortable to wear. However, those who wore the ear defenders on a regular basis reported that the initial discomfort fairly soon wore off, and that if they then had to remove them, they became uncomfortably aware of the magnitude of the noise in the shed. In fact, many of this minority would not now enter the weaving shed without their ear defenders.

The method adopted to improve this situation was to reward the wearing of ear defenders using tokens. These tokens could be saved and exchanged for goods that were displayed in cabinets in the sheds. The workforce was told of the nature of the scheme, its start date and the date at which it would finish. The project actually lasted two months. It was also made clear that there was no compulsion to take part and that non-wearers would not be subject to sanctions. In order to provide the variable ratio reinforcement element of the scheme, tokens were distributed three times a week, on a 'quasi-random' basis. A token was given to each individual actually wearing ear defenders at the time the distribution was made. No exceptions were made, or excuses accepted. Care was taken to ensure that no advance warning of an imminent token distribution could occur. In order to help overcome the initial discomfort of wearing the defenders, time bands of increasing length, during which token distribution would take place, were defined. For the first three days distribution was sometime during the first two hours of each shift; during the next three days it was during the first four hours, and so on. Within these time bands the distribution was on a totally random basis.

The effect of this approach was to produce dramatic change. Within the first week ear defender usage rose to effectively 100 per cent and remained there throughout the whole of the two-month period during which tokens were distributed. Even when token distribution ceased, the level of usage remained at the same high level and continued to do so on random follow-up visits a year later. What had happened at this stage was that ear defender wearing had become self-reinforcing. Workers now found the high noise levels experienced when they removed the defenders punishing and were negatively reinforced (by the removal of the unpleasant noise) when they put them back on again.

CONTROLLING A MANAGER'S WORKLOAD

The problem for this middle manager was that he was feeling severely stressed and overworked. He was working late hours, which was having a detrimental effect on his family life. He was also suffering from insomnia which he though was work related. In addition he was getting behind with tasks his boss was giving him. His boss was complaining more and more about missed deadlines. Like other managers his tasks came from three sources. Some tasks were generated by his boss and some were self-generated. He was also under the impression that many of his tasks were generated by the shop-floor staff who worked for him. He had a number of supervisors, who had direct responsibility for these workers, but he liked to see himself as a 'hands-on' manager, in touch with shop-floor problems. He, in fact, enjoyed this inter-personal and problem solving aspect of his job.

Analysis of the behaviour

As a start on the process of solving his problem of work overload the manager undertook a two-week analysis of the number of tasks he had to do, and where they originated. The findings were:

Boss generated	17
Self-generated	20
Subordinate-generated	84

The high number of tasks that he was undertaking that were subordinate generated came as quite a surprise, particularly as he had supervisors who could (and probably should) have been dealing with many of them.

Functional analysis of the manager's behaviour and that of his subordinates suggested that, for the subordinates, it was the manager's arrival on the shop floor that was the cue that led to the raising of problems. This behaviour would have been reinforced by the manager taking responsibility for dealing with these problems. In addition, this was further reinforced by social attention from the manager, who was popular and well liked. In analysing his own behaviour the manager realized that he enjoyed dealing with, and solving, the subordinate-generated problems. In addition he liked being liked! Hence, he was receiving strong reinforcement, which was keeping this behaviour going.

The solution

As with many behavioural problems, measurement is often part of the solution. As noted above, it came as quite a surprise to the manager that so much of his workload was subordinate generated. Although he gained reinforcement from solving these problems he realized that this was not what a manager should be doing. The supervisors should have been dealing with most of these problems. He decided, therefore, to use discriminant stimuli (see Chapter 3) with his subordinates. If they approached him with a problem he would listen whilst they described the details. This provided social reinforcement for both the manager and the subordinate. Rather than dealing with the problem himself, however, he would direct the person to the appropriate supervisor. Only if he thought it was his direct responsibility did he offer to deal with the problem.

Results

The results are shown graphically in Figure 5.1. The plots for the first two weeks show the baseline figures, when the subordinate generated tasks were very significantly higher than those generated by the boss or the manager himself. The figures for weeks 3 to 6 are for the intervention stage. As can be seen, by week 6 the total number of tasks has more than halved, mainly because the number of subordinate-generated tasks has fallen by three-quarters. The intervention has succeeded dramatically. It may be that the supervisors are now experiencing an increased workload, but it is possible that they were underutilized before, as the manager was dealing with many of the problems that should have been within their remit.

This example shows how very simple, and it might be thought, obvious techniques can be used to great effect. It may be thought that the solution was obvious to any intelligent person, but in response it may be said that this problem had been ongoing, and getting worse, for some months. It would not surprise us if there were many other managers experiencing very similar problems. The beauty of this solution is that managers can implement it for themselves without cost or the need to involve others.

The three examples given above show how the principles of behaviour modification can be used to solve three different types of group management problem. In the first a new manager is confronted with the problem of improving the performance of a group of professional engineers, who are significantly under-performing. In the second a large group are all influenced to make one small but important change – to wear ear defenders. In the third a manager increases his effectiveness by changing the way his subordinates relate to him. What is significant here is that by making a small change in

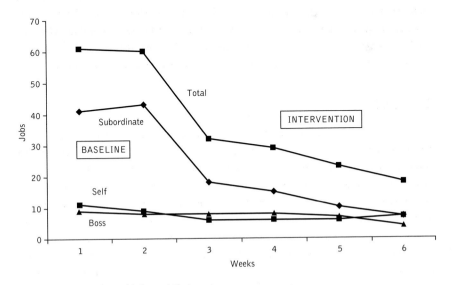

Figure 5.1 *Number of jobs and their source*

his own behaviour, the manager has created an important change in his subordinates' behaviour. These changes were all made using the classic behavioural approach of specifying the behaviour required, measuring the current baseline and reinforcing the required behaviour. Knowing the baseline levels enables the amount of change to be measured.

The above examples are all cases were a manager is *reacting* to an existing situation in order to create an improvement in performance. While this is a quite common occurrence there are other occasions when a manager is expected to be *proactive*. In this situation the manager is expected to be 'ahead of the game' and to be creating the conditions for outstanding performance. This is what is often thought of as *leadership*.

MANAGEMENT AND LEADERSHIP

The management literature has for several decades been concerned with the issue of the relationship between *management* and *leadership*. Whether this has been of quite such concern to practising managers is another question. This discussion has often revolved around the issue of proactive versus reactive, mentioned above. With leaders seen as proactive and managers reactive. Zaleznik (1977), for example, has argued, somewhat along these lines, suggesting that managers and leaders exhibit very different characteristics. These differences are summarized in Box 5.1. Others, usually in more general management textbooks, write as if the terms are synonymous: managers and leaders being essentially the same. Achieving clarity is also made more difficult by the tendency to confuse the way in which the words 'leadership', 'management' and 'supervision' are used in different texts. They are often used almost interchangeably. This is, no doubt, partly because they denote complex ideas that are hard to define precisely, and which do, in any case, have some overlap. Another problem is that they are also sometimes used to refer to a role – as in 'the management': a function of the organization, and at other times to refer to a process – as in managing the team, i.e. controlling it and getting it to work.

In this context we are here concerned with leadership as a process. The view we take is very similar to that originally put forward by Mintzberg (1973). Namely, that to be a leader is one part, and only one part, of a manager's job. Mintzberg's research, admittedly based on rather a small sample, suggests that a manager has many roles, only one of which is leadership (the complete set of roles is listed in Box 5.2). However, leadership is a very important aspect of a manager's interpersonal roles, and one that can be developed using the behavioural approach.

Before going further we need to define a little more precisely what we mean by the term leadership. Essentially, it is concerned with what managers actually do to help the group carry out its tasks and achieve its objectives. Most definitions include at least the four following functions:

Box 5.1:
MANAGERS AND LEADERS

Zaleznik (1977) suggested that there are very significant differences between managers and leaders in their approach to work in organizations. He saw managers as tending towards being conservative, rule bound and strategic, whereas leaders were seen as more intuitive, higher-risk takers and driven by their own, rather than organizational values. The following table summarizes these differences in three relevant areas: relations with others, goals and conception of work.

Relations with others

Managers	traditional and conservative work through the 'system' constrained by role.
Leaders	intuitive and empathic direct communication higher risk.

Goals

Managers	goals arise from organizational necessity focus on strategy.
Leaders	goals arise from values strategy is means to a goal.

Conception of work

Managers	value tradition analytical and methodical maintain control identify with organization.
Leaders	seek change and new ideas intuitive encourage autonomy more independent.

Box 5.2:
MINTZBERG'S MANAGERIAL ROLES

Based on detailed observation of the work of a group of chief executives Mintzberg (1973) defined 10 roles which are an integral part of managerial work. These divide into three groups: those concerned with the interactions of people within the group, information handling roles and decision-making. The 10 roles are listed below.

Interpersonal roles
Figurehead
Leader
Liaison

Informational roles
Monitor
Disseminator
Spokesperson

Decision-making roles
Entrepreneur
Disturbance handler
Resource allocator
Negotiator

Defining the task: making clear what has to be done;

Managing the process: defining, or helping the group to evolve, rules and procedures and ensuring that they are applied;

Managing the boundary: representing the group externally both outwardly and inwardly;

Group development: developing and mobilizing the full resources within the group.

In what follows we are concerned with how effectively managers achieve these functions.

Early research on leadership

Much of the earliest research on leadership took the form of comparing the characteristics of leaders compared with those that they were leading and was usually in non-organizational contexts (such as Scout groups). The results were often inconclusive although some general trends did emerge. Leaders tended to be more intelligent, higher on self-confidence, originality and influence than their followers. No great surprises there, and only worth mentioning because there has been a recent trend for studies of business leaders in an attempt to define their characteristics (sometimes disparagingly referred to as 'great man' studies). While these have produced some interesting findings they are not usually couched in behavioural terms and so do not tell us much about how to improve leadership behaviour.

Moving on from this basic approach research began to focus on trying to answer two fundamental questions:

1 What do effective leaders *do*?
2 What do effective leaders *do differently* that distinguishes them from less effective leaders?

Unfortunately, however, the job descriptions of different managers vary considerably, therefore the tasks and behaviours of these different managers will also vary considerably. Given this variety any overall theory of leadership has to categorize these specific behaviours into more general categories. Two studies which started on this path were carried out at the Ohio State University and the University of Michigan, respectively.

The Ohio State studies

One of the earliest studies to look at leadership in, at least quasi-behavioural terms was carried out at the Ohio State University in the 1950s. The researchers collected a large number of statements from employees about their manager's or supervisor's behaviour. When analysed these were shown to fall into two broad and largely independent categories.

Consideration: defined as the degree of friendship, warmth, trust and respect shown by the supervisor to subordinates.

Initiating structure: the degree to which the supervisor defines his/her own role, and what is expected of individual subordinates and defines the organization and patterns of communication.

The Michigan studies

At very much the same time as the Ohio State studies, similar work was being carried out at the University of Michigan, with very similar results. The dimensions found in this case were:

Production or task oriented behaviour: the supervisor concentrates on the practicalities of production, making sure that schedules are maintained and production targets are met.

> *Person or relationship oriented behaviour*: the supervisor concentrates on the welfare of subordinates and on maintaining good relationships.

It is clear that the two studies produced very similar findings as there is considerable overlap in the two sets of dimensions. Also in both studies the two dimensions were reasonably independent, i.e. a particular manager could be high on either one and low on the other or high or low on both. Research was carried out on the importance of each dimension for effective management. The current received wisdom is that both are important and the effective manager should be high on both, although each dimension might require a different emphasis in different contexts. Many other theories and classifications of leadership behaviour have since been suggested, some based on observation and data collection and others more philosophical in nature. The majority can be seen as extensions and elaborations of the two original studies at Ohio State and Michigan Universities.

A BEHAVIOURAL APPROACH TO LEADERSHIP

More recent research by Komaki and her associates starts from a precise view of successful managerial leadership behaviour. For example, Komaki (1998) states that an effective manager will 'make appropriate behaviours clear, accurately and fairly appraise performance and provide consequences contingent upon performance'. This is reminiscent of the standard antecedents–behaviour–consequences sequence of traditional behaviour modification. It will be recalled from Chapter 3 that in behavioural theory *behaviour is a function of its consequences*. Whether a behaviour will continue or cease will be largely influenced by the consequences that follow the behaviour. We have also seen, however, that behaviour is also influenced by the antecedents that precede it. These antecedents, or cues, initiate a behaviour. This produces the ABC mnemonic – *antecedents* trigger *behaviour* which produces *consequences*. It is these three categories, which together are unique to the behavioural theory, which is used to analyse leadership. Researchers, such as Komaki (1998) have made considerable progress using this approach. However, there is one additional category that needs to be added. This extra category is required because a manager does not, as a rule, carry out the same tasks as those of the people he is managing. The manager's job is to prescribe, co-ordinate and monitor the tasks carried out, rather than do them himself. This means that additional element that has to be added to the behavioural 'equation' is that of *monitoring* the behaviour of others. As we will see, *monitoring*, together with *consequences*, according to Komaki's research, form the cornerstones of behavioural leadership. Before considering the relative importance of each of the elements, however, we perhaps need to consider each of them in a little more detail as they apply to leadership.

100

Antecedents

In everyday life most of the antecedents that initiate (or in some cases inhibit) behaviour go largely unrecognized. They are often subtle and unstated. In the case of work-related behaviours, however, they may be explicit and formally stated, although not always, even in this context. Often we do need to know precisely what is required of us at work and we know this by making the relationship between cues and the behaviours required explicit: as in 'Take *a*, do *b* to it, and place it in *c*'. Rules, instructions, procedures and the like, are antecedents; they specify what needs to be done when a particular cue is encountered. Some jobs, of course, require training in order to do them effectively. Much of training is getting people to recognize cues and learning what behaviour is required when they are encountered. Indeed, much of the 'experience' we acquire when we do jobs for a long time is a matter of learning finer and finer discrimination of the cues and the behaviours required. One of the trademarks of a highly skilled worker is that they will often notice subtle differences in cues that a novice would not. For example, before the introduction of computer controlled production in steelworks, it was the foreman's job to decide when the hot steel was ready to roll. He did this by the smelling the steel! This skill only came with years of experience and was apparently related to the changing sulphur content on the steel during its heating.

The manager is usually a major source of these work-related antecedents. They provide instructions, whether verbal or written. They create or amend procedures and they set goals, which can also be seen as an antecedent that indicates their expectations of their subordinates' performance.

Monitoring

Monitoring perhaps needs less explanation than antecedents. Its use in behavioural theory is similar to its everyday usage, i.e. checking what someone (usually a subordinate) is doing. Monitoring is essentially a data collection exercise and consists of the collection, either before or after performance, of performance-related information. In research there are three common methods of monitoring: work sampling, self-report and secondary sources such as production figures and reports from third parties. In practice, in work situations the most common methods are direct observation and production data. One problem that can arise with monitoring is that subordinates occasionally see this as interference or complain that they feel that the boss is continually checking up on them. This can be avoided so long as the monitoring is done openly and objectively, and the subordinate understands what is going on. Some hints on how to achieve effective monitoring are given later in this chapter.

Consequences

Throughout this book much emphasis has been placed on the significance of consequences, and their effect as reinforcement or punishment of the preceding behaviour. While most of the familiar reinforcers apply in the context of behavioural leadership, it will be no surprise to learn that two of the most powerful and important reinforcers are again feedback and recognition. We are social animals who need social acceptance so it could be expected that recognition, and attention, are perhaps the most powerful of reinforcers. Feedback on the other hand is not immediately obvious as a source of reinforcement. We have noted earlier, however, that feedback can have a powerful influence on behaviour. This is particularly so if it satisfies the PIGS acronym, i.e. it is positive, immediate, graphic and specific. An interesting insight on the relationship between money and other more social forms of reinforcement is provided by Stajkovic and Luthans (2001). In a study over a period of one month, with admittedly rather small samples (ranging from 39 to 50), supervisors who had not been trained in behavioural techniques obtained an 11 per cent improvement in performance from their subordinates. Supervisors who were trained in the behavioural approach and using only social (e.g. recognition) or feedback as reinforcers obtained improvements in performance ranging from 20 per cent to 24 per cent. However, one group, trained in behavioural techniques and using financial reward as reinforcement, did obtain an improvement of 31 per cent. This provides some evidence for the value of training supervisors in behaviour analysis and shows that significant improvements in performance can be obtained with purely social reinforcement; but that money, appropriately used, is also a significant form of reinforcement.

In other contexts that we have discussed, feedback has been provided in the form of graphs and charts, usually prominently displayed in the workplace. (See the safety programme in Chapter 6 for example.) This is a good way of providing feedback information at a group level. For individuals, as when a manager is dealing directly with a subordinate, verbal feedback on a one-to-one basis is more likely to be effective. There is, incidentally, clear evidence that it is best to avoid evaluative feedback. Research suggests that it is not necessary for the manager to imply approval or disapproval of an action, but what is crucially important is for the manager's knowledge of performance to be *transmitted* to the person concerned. Knowledge of performance (i.e. feedback) itself can be considered to be a consequence.

BEHAVIOURAL LEADERSHIP IN PRACTICE

In our experience managers (and others) find the terms *antecedents*, *monitoring* and *consequences* rather technical and not user-friendly. We have, therefore, suggested an alternative terminology using plainer language. We find this makes much clearer what is meant by each of these terms.

Antecedents, it will be recalled, are instructions as to what needs to be done, and how. These instructions may be verbal or written. In terms of what a manager *does*, therefore, we would suggest that antecedents involve *telling* or *instructing*.

Monitoring involves the collection of information, whether it is directly from the employee, or from other sources. Monitoring, therefore, involves *asking* or *enquiring*.

This enquiring may be a request for information from records (e.g. concerning production output or maintenance) but more commonly it entails such simple requests as 'how's the task going?'

Finding an appropriate everyday term for *consequences* we have found more difficult. The essential feature of consequences is that knowledge or evaluation of performance must be transmitted to the employee concerned. It is not necessary that it is evaluative; knowledge alone is considered a consequence. Transmitting such knowledge involves *feedback* which, as we have seen, is a powerful reinforcer. Consequences also usually involve *commenting* on performance in some way.

Rather than AMC sequences, therefore, we can now talk about managers:

- telling/instructing
- asking/enquiring, and
- commenting/giving feedback.

This is, of course a cycle. Commenting and giving feedback may well lead to new or modified instructions (see Figure 5.2).

Using this new terminology for Komaki's findings the advice for leaders becomes somewhat clearer. Her central finding that what differentiates good leaders from the not so good is that the good leaders monitor, translates as *good leaders do a lot of asking*. Lack-lustre leaders are more detached and uninvolved. They do not go to their subordinates and *ask*.

Not only do good leaders do more asking, but the order in which they do it is important. Good leaders *ask/enquire before they tell/instruct*. Komaki found that poor leaders, on the other hand, *tell before they ask*. This difference is crucial. Being asked before being instructed is likely to produce a far more positive response than being told before being asked. Asking about job-related activities stimulates people to talk about their performance. This in turn sets the stage for more performance-related, give-and-

Effective leaders' behaviours				Supervisory effectiveness
Telling/asking/commenting sequences composed of				
Telling conveying expectations of performance	*Asking* gathering performance information	*Commenting* indicating knowledge of performance using combination of positive, negative, and neutral consequences	leads to	Higher performance and Positive attitudes about supervisor
Which stimulates dialogue between leader and follower about what follower has done				

Figure 5.2 *A behavioural model of effective leadership*
Source: adapted from Komaki (1998)

take exchanges. In addition, the act of asking gives some indication of task importance. We naturally concentrate on what is important.

So, in order to be a good leader:

- managers need to interact with their subordinates
- such interactions have to be about performance-related issues
- an important element of such interactions is asking/enquiring.

Stated simply this sounds obvious, but it is surprising how often this advice is not followed. Managers often seem to avoid contact with their subordinates. This may be because such contact raises problems, which is punishment for the manager. They then have a tendency to tell rather than ask, whereas asking may elicit information that will help to solve the problem. By contrast, reference back to the problem of the under-performing engineers at the beginning of this chapter will show that the process we recommend was used. The manager spent time talking to individual engineers specifying performance requirements and then monitored progress, again by personal contact and questioning. Finally, reinforcement was provided, mainly in the form of feedback, but also recognition.

It is interesting to note, in passing, that there is a connection with the Ohio State and Michigan studies in the above advice. The need for a manager to relate to people but concentrate on performance echoes the view that a good manager needs to be both person and task oriented. We find it encouraging when studies coming from different directions produce complementary findings. It is even better when, as in this case, the later study adds refinement and detail.

We can now move to give even more precise advice about the process of asking/enquiring.

How to ask/enquire

The basic building blocks of any information-gathering exercise are questions and one of the quickest ways of increasing the effectiveness of this process is to be able to choose the correct type of question. First, however, we have to be able to recognize the different types and be aware of their uses. Table 5.1 lists some of different types of questions. As an exercise, first familiarize yourself with them, and then analyse some real-life interactions. Any such interaction will do, but we find that the following are often useful in highlighting certain questioning techniques. Compare any 'chat show' host, with more searching interviews. Some of the best of these may be found in cross-examinations of politicians by political correspondents. You will find it informative to compare the sort of information elicited by the different types of question. This will also show why some interviewers are more effective than others.

Each of the first four question types listed in Table 5.1 has its particular uses. The most effective way of opening an interaction whose main objective is information gathering

Table 5.1 Types of question

Type of question	Useful for	Not useful for
Open 'Tell me what happened when . . .'	Most openings Exploring and gathering information on a broad basis	Very talkative interviewee
Closed 'How many widgets did you produce?'	Getting specific, factual answers	Getting broadly-based information
Probing 'For precisely how long did you do that?'	Establishing and checking details of events already known or arising from the answers to open questions	Exploring emotionally charged areas
Hypothetical 'What would you do if . . . happened?'	Getting people to think in broader terms, or about a new area	If the hypothesized situation is outside the person's experience
Multiple A string of questions or statements	Never useful	Never useful

Source: adapted from Randell *et al.* (1984)

is to use an *open* question, with the general structure 'tell me about . . .'. The beauty of such questions is that they can elicit a large amount of useful information and give the manager an overview of what's happening. The initial use of an open question also has some other advantages. Open questions are less threatening, especially if things have been going wrong, as they allow the subordinate to paint the picture from their perspective. An open question, for example, may elicit from an individual an indication of how much they felt they were responsible. In addition, they may also indicate the extent to which they have already learnt from the events. It may be that they are already taking the necessary corrective action. The use of an open question also indicates that the manager has an open mind and is keen to get all the information before making a judgement. This avoids defensive behaviour on the part of the subordinate. The immediate reaction to attack, in the form of a pre-judgement of 'guilt' on the part of the manager, is defence. Under these conditions the subordinate will be unlikely to admit to any fault on their part, for fear that the admission will be used to press the attack even further. The tactic becomes one of defending the outer lines, only falling back when absolutely necessary. Such interactions are not likely to be very productive.

Although the question types described may be used on their own they are also, not surprisingly, often found in combination. One sequencing of questions that is particularly appropriate for information gathering has been referred to as the funnel technique – so called because the information gathered becomes more and more specific as the sequence proceeds.

Using this technique the discussion about the events in question starts with an open question, for the reasons discussed above. A problem with using an open question, however, is that it may produce information that is not specific enough and lacking in depth. In order to elicit more detailed information, probes may be used. For example, 'whom did you consult about stopping the production line?' The answer to this question will be more detailed but may still omit specific relevant information. If this is so it may be necessary to follow the probe with a closed question in order to produce answers to specific points. For example, 'did you get authority from the Production Manager to stop the line?' Finally, it is often useful to use a summary to check that your information is correct. As you may be interested in a number of job-related events, it is not unusual to find this cycle of open, probing, and closed questions, together with summaries, being repeated as different events are discussed.

The most important single piece of advice that can be given to managers who want to improve their asking/enquiring skills is: *start any performance-related interaction with a subordinate with an open question.* (This is especially important when things have gone wrong.) We would also suggest two other things you as a manager should do:

Monitor the amount of time you spend interacting with your subordinates about performance-related matters.

Monitor the number of times you start a performance-related interaction with an open question.

It is likely that you will wish to increase both these behaviours and you will, therefore, need to develop a strategy to encourage them. Think about what is reinforcing your present behaviour and what you can do to reinforce the new desired activity.

Rules, regulations and reinforcement

A practical problem for managers is that while they control a number of elements in the ABC sequence, there are some over which they may have little or no influence. It may not be possible, for example, to control all the subtle and implicit antecedents that influence people's behaviour. Likewise, consequences are often intrinsic to the job and also subjective (for example under the Premack principle individuals will be differently reinforced by the sequence of their more or less preferred tasks). Relating to this is a finding concerning the amount of time managers devote to each of the three categories of behaviour: antecedents, monitoring and consequences. In a study that reviewed 10 years of research, Daniels (1989) found that managers spend, on average, approximately 80 per cent of their time on activities that can be classed as antecedents (e.g. creating and modifying procedures, defining tasks and giving instructions). This obviously means they are spending much less time on monitoring and consequences, which are, therefore, relatively neglected. The fact that managers, on average, spend most of their time on antecedents suggests that this behaviour is being reinforced. The reinforcement may, of course, be either external (reinforcers generated by the organization), or internal (subjective reinforcers and those intrinsic to the task itself). We suspect that both are at work.

Most organizations have a framework of rules and regulations of varying degrees of size and complexity. This is such a widespread phenomena that the occasional organization that attempts to develop alternative ways of working usually attracts a great deal of attention and comment. Semler (1994) describes, for example, how in a large engineering company he withdrew all procedure manuals and flow charts and encouraged people to manage by 'common sense'. Employees were, apparently, confused at first and wanted to know when new manuals were to be issued, but slowly 'cottoned on' and began to work on their own initiative. At the time, certainly the company was, by Semler's own account, doing very well. Whilst it is undeniable that rules and regulations are required in order to run very complex organizations, rule books do have their downside and some organizational theorists are suggesting that the balance has shifted too far towards 'rules' rather than good management (or common sense).

In his Presidential Address to the British Psychological Society, Chris Cullen (1998) commented on this, pointing out the stultifying effect rules can have on creativity and innovation. The effect of rules is to place a heavy emphasis on compliance with associated monitoring, usually involving the generation of large numbers of documents. This process, at best, leads to staff following rigid routines to ensure the avoidance of mistakes, for which they may be punished. At worst it can lead to falsification of records and low morale. Because staff are spending so much time following rules they tend to lose sight of the primary objective of the organization. As a result production and/or quality suffers. This in turn leads to management creating more rules to try and rectify this situation. Thus the cycle starts again. This process is illustrated in Figure 5.3.

The fact that so much time and energy is spent on developing and following rules and regulations implies that there must be some quite powerful reinforcers at work. Some of it may be intrinsic satisfaction – we feel we have been efficient when we have produced a nice set of rules. Also it makes us feel safe – things are under control. There may be an historical and cultural foundation for this – most organizations in the past were bureaucracies (most large ones still are today) so we have a belief that this is how to run organizations. Once we have regulations, there is a fear of punishment if we do not follow them. There are inevitably sanctions of some sort built in, ranging from the threat of dismissal to loss of privileges or resources. It is this threat of punishment that can lead to falsification to avoid the sanctions

There is a possibility that other intrinsic, subjective reinforcers are at work. Recalling the Premack principle, it may that many managers actually prefer to deal with paper rather than people. In other words, dealing with administrative procedures is higher up their hierarchy than personal interaction. We have some indirect evidence of this from

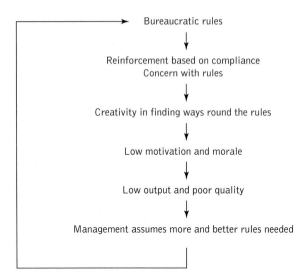

Figure 5.3 *Effect of rules*

projects carried out by managers on our courses. It is not unusual for us to get projects where managers, who have realized that they do not have enough personal contact with their subordinates and peers, try to increase this by going to see people rather than, for example, using e-mail. The likelihood is, of course, that all these reinforcers are influencing managers' behaviour. Whatever the reinforcers, however, the fact remains that managers appear to spend much of their time engaged in behaviours associated with antecedents.

This, in our experience, is common in high-tech companies, where managers are promoted because of their technical competence. They eventually reach a level where their main task is to deal with people, but they really much prefer to be working with their original technology. Hence they escape back to the 'workbench' whenever possible. We have called this the 'reluctant manager syndrome'.

Developing effective supervisors

To conclude this chapter we will return to the problem of persuading operators to wear ear defenders. We described above the work done by Zohar and Fussfeld (1981) in using behavioural techniques to increase ear defender usage in a noisy factory. More recently Dov Zohar (2002) has used behavioural leadership techniques as an alternative approach to achieve the same end. In this case there were 381 workers and 36 supervisors who were undertaking the repair, maintenance and upgrading of heavy-duty equipment. As in the previous study the use of ear defenders was low, with only 25 per cent of the workers wearing them. The difference between this case and that discussed earlier is that, instead of trying to influence the workers' behaviour directly, they trained the supervisors in the techniques of behavioural management. The essential feature of behavioural leadership is that it involves the supervisor communicating with the workers about work-related issues. In this case the particular work-related behaviour being safety behaviours.

In order to establish how much work-related communications were currently taking place researchers questioned a sample of workers on a random basis, using 'backward recall' interviews. These interviews asked workers to recall the work they had done over last few hours. This was repeated going back further in time, until the workers could not remember any more. These interviews average 3–5 minutes and the amount that workers could recall covered an average span of 2–3 days. They were then asked to describe work-related interactions with their supervisor. Following the interviews, the researchers classified the workers' descriptions of their interactions (including non-verbal elements) with their supervisors as to whether they were: safety-related, production-related, or both. This was carried out over a period of three months to establish the baseline. Safety-oriented interactions averaged 9 per cent over the baseline period. This was followed by an eight-week intervention period during which supervisors were told that their safety-oriented interactions with the workers were being measured and they were given feedback on an individual basis. (Managers were also given feedback, but only on a comparative basis so as to avoid any possible punishment for individual supervisors.)

During the intervention stage safety-oriented episodes increased from the 9 per cent of the baseline to a plateau averaging 58 per cent, which was maintained five months later. The fact that this increase was maintained over such a long period, most probably means that the behaviour had become a habit, with its own, inherent, reinforcers. The effect on earplug usage was also impressive, rising from the baseline of 25 per cent to a plateau averaging 73 per cent. This also was maintained five months later. In order to ensure that the beneficial effects did not fade with time managers were trained to use the interview technique and to give feedback to their supervisors as a permanent working practice.

It can be hypothesized that as the feedback process continues, the supervisors' interactions with their subordinates will continue to improve, with consequent further increase in ear defender use.

In the next chapter we discuss how the principles of behaviour analysis can be extended to managing across the total organization, particularly in relation to creating large-scale organizational change.

CHAPTER SUMMARY

This chapter commenced with some examples of how the behavioural approach can be effectively used with groups of individuals. This is done by applying the same techniques as those used for individual change but extending them across a whole department or work group. There followed a discussion of the difference between management and leadership leading to the suggestion that leadership is but one of many roles which a manager has to undertake, albeit a very important one. A relatively new, but important, area of research is concerned with the behavioural approach to leadership.

Much of this research has been carried out by Komaki (1998), and her colleagues, who developed a very comprehensive technique for recording what leaders actually do. The research is very detailed and thorough, and the results are very clear as to what leaders do, and what distinguishes effective leaders from their less effective colleagues. As in any major research programme, there were many findings, but the single most important factor that separates effective from less effective managers is the extent to which they engage in *monitoring*. Effective managers are more involved in monitoring, particularly in relation to work performance. In practical terms this is best achieved by *asking/enquiring*. In particular the use of open questions is a technique that managers can easily use to initiate monitoring. Such monitoring is not just a passive activity; a manager who is monitoring is also *interacting* and *communicating* with his subordinates about *their performance*. This communication sets in operation a sequence of events that leads to effective leadership. During the process managers gain useful information about work-related performance, which allows them to provide rapid consequences of all kinds, positive, negative, and neutral. The information given to the subordinate need not be evaluative, but if necessary, may be. This form of the manager–subordinate interaction encourages performance-related give-and-take exchanges, which stimulates subordinates to review and talk about their performance. Thus, monitoring leads to managers providing consequences, and to subordinates reviewing and discussing their own performance. This sequence of behaviours tends to be self-replicating, thus leading to a continuous process of review and improvement.

One factor which has a strong influence on the antecedents–monitoring–consequences cycle is the heavy emphasis, in many organizations, on antecedents, in the form of rules and regulations. In some organizations this is so marked that it implies that quite strong reinforcers must be involved. The danger of this situation is that rewarding conformity to rules tends to inhibit creativity and innovation.

Chapter 6

Managing at the organizational level

It is sometimes assumed that behaviour analysis is not a suitable technique for making organizational change interventions. This seems to be based on the belief that because the approach involves defining specific behaviours of individuals it can only be used to change individual behaviour. We have seen in the previous chapter that this is, in fact, not true. It is sometimes further suggested that any major change in organizational culture involves a re-appraisal of the way that individuals perceive the organization and that such a cognitive re-organization is outside the scope of this methodology. For this reason many OD projects involve complex plans for the structure and culture of the changed organization and then set up elaborate programmes to train people in new procedures and to change attitudes. As we suggested in Chapter 2, the latter is very difficult, if not impossible, to do. However, all organizational change obviously depends, at root, on behaviour change on the part of individual members of the organization and, as we have seen in previous chapters, the behavioural approach is an ideal method for bringing about such change. There is also evidence that once behaviour has changed attitudes and perceptions will also adjust in line. The following case study illustrates how the behavioural approach was very successfully used in a major change intervention.

CULTURE CHANGE IN A CONTINUOUS PROCESS PLANT

The OBMod continuous safety improvement programme

The intervention described here was carried out by the authors, in conjunction with several colleagues over a period of five years. (We would particularly like to acknowledge the influence on this project of our colleague Dr Valerie Sutherland.) The initial assignment was to increase safety in the plant but was later extended, at the request of the management, to include quality improvement, and ultimately created considerable change in the culture of the organization including a high degree of real empowerment at all levels of the workforce.

The factory was part of a large multinational organization operating in the paper-making industry. The production process ran on a continuous shift system that operated on a ten-day cycle. There was a workforce of approximately 550. Although the majority of these were in the 'core' production process, they were supported by various maintenance and administrative staff. These included 'blue-collar' departments such as engineering maintenance, and 'white-collar' departments, predominantly offices. With one minor exception, the intervention involved all the organization's employees on site. There was an active commitment to safety throughout the organization, but particularly at senior management level. The site had a full-time safety officer and an active safety committee that included both shop-floor and management representatives. In the past, efforts to improve safety had been reactive rather than proactive, involving correcting dangerous situations after accidents had occurred. These efforts had been very successful at reducing lost time accidents (LTAs) but the company was having difficulty in reducing minor accidents below a fairly steady baseline level.

As the purpose of the initial stage of the project was to use the behavioural approach to improve safety and the safety culture of the organization, a number of key principles on which the intervention would be based were established at the outset. These were:

- a concentration on safe behaviour, rather than attitudes, in the belief that this was the way to reduce accidents. Any subsequent change in attitudes would be a consequence and not the cause of safe behaviour;
- the reinforcement of safe behaviour rather than the punishment and discipline of unsafe behaviours;
- measuring safe behaviour not hazards;
- accepting that the best people to identify safe behaviour are the operators themselves;
- training operators to observe and measure safe behaviour, provide visual feedback and praise to reinforce the desired safe behaviours;
- the workforce to set its own goals and observe its own behaviour.

A fairly structured five-step process of behaviour change, adapted from by Luthans and Kreitner (1985), was used as a basic model for this intervention. This included:

1 Identify the key behaviour involved.
2 Measure the baseline frequency of the key behaviour.
3 Set goals for improvement in desired behaviour.
4 Intervene by feedback and reinforcement to increase the frequency of desired behaviour and reduce the frequency of undesirable behaviour.
5 Evaluate to determine whether or not behaviour and performance have changed in the desired direction.

The method of measuring the desired behaviour and providing feedback was via checklists devised and applied by the participants themselves, although it was recognized that some help in developing the initial checklists would have to be provided by the consultants.

Before the start of any organizational change programme it is usually necessary to undertake some 'awareness raising' activities. In this case raising the profile of safety issues helped the implementation of the behavioural programme itself. This awareness raising was accomplished in a variety of ways. A number of briefings were given to senior members of the organization (i.e. those concerned with making the decision that the project should proceed), explaining the theory underlying the approach and outlining the stages of the project. When the decision had definitely been made to go ahead, a letter of intent, signed by the chief executive, was sent to all employees. This stated the aims and objectives of the programme and was intended to signal that there was a high level of commitment to it at the most senior levels of the organization. This was backed up with notices on bulletin boards and items in company newsletters. The consultants then gave a series of briefings to all personnel who were ultimately going to be involved. These explained the underlying theory of the behavioural approach and outlined what was going to happen during the intervention itself.

Having set appropriate expectations and, as far as possible clarified misunderstandings and concerns among the workforce, the next stage was to implement various diagnostic procedures. A safety climate questionnaire was circulated throughout the factory to gain views on a variety of aspects associated with the safety culture and the working environment. The survey produced a 70 per cent response rate and the results were helpful as a guide to structure the implementation of the intervention. Following this a series of in-depth semi-structured interviews was conducted with a sample of 70 people (15 per cent of the workforce). These interviews aimed to reveal minor accidents, which often go unreported, and to gain an idea of the behaviour that caused them. An analysis of the previous 24 months of accident records was also carried out to identify patterns of unsafe behaviour. This revealed a number of unsafe practices, such as, blocked doorways, items left in gangways and failure to wear appropriate protective clothing in certain situations.

After this diagnostic stage, we were able to start work on the actual intervention. The procedure was as follows:

- Checklists of the behaviours most commonly associated with accidents were generated using data from the above diagnostic techniques. Draft checklists were produced and refined in consultation with departmental managers and safety committee members. Figure 6.1 gives an example of one of the final departmental checklists.
- A total of 48 observers was needed to observe across all departments and all shift patterns. The first group of 'volunteer' observers was 'selected' to include safety committee members, some supervisors and some people known to show an interest in safety. They attended a two-day training programme in using the checklists and monitoring the behaviour of their peers. The first day of the training programme included the theory and principles of the behavioural approach that emphasized reward rather than punishment and the use of praise and feedback as

	OBSERVATION 1			OBSERVATION 2		
	100% SAFE	UNSAFE	NOT SEEN	100% SAFE	UNSAFE	NOT SEEN
1 Floor/walkways/ steps/stairs free of tripping/slipping hazards						
2 Dye or chemical spillage to be treated immediately						
3 Machine chests to be kept clear of obstructions						
4 Safety footwear to be worn at all times						
5 Ear protection to be worn in designated areas						
6 Eye protection to be worn when handling chemicals						
7 Gloves to be worn when handling chemicals and dyes						
8 Eye wash station seals not broken						
9 Hoses to be coiled/stored when not in use						
10 Caustic chains in place when caustic in use						
11 Protective clothing used when handling caustic						
12 Dye and chemical stocks stored in designated areas						
13 Fork truck to be used in accordance with mill procedures						
14 Pallet trucks to be parked in designated areas when not in use						
15 Lock-off procedures to be observed						
16 Fire exits clear						
17 Fire extinguishers in place/seals not broken						
18 Access to fire hose and extinguishers to be kept clear						
Totals:						
Percentages:						

Figure 6.1 *Example of a safety behaviour checklist*

reinforcement. The training also covered techniques needed to run the sessions where safety targets would be set. On the second day of the training the observers were taught how to use and score the checklists and practised with the checklists on the factory floor. The lists were modified as necessary on the basis of these practical experiences

- Four weeks of observations followed the training period in order to establish a baseline measure. With practice the observers were able to complete the checks, on average, in about ten minutes. The data was gathered centrally and used to calculate a baseline figure for safe behaviour. This was expressed as the number of safe behaviours out of all the behaviours observed, and took into account the percentage of behaviours 'not seen'. Enlarged copies of the checklists were displayed in all departments.

- At the end of the four-week baseline period all employees attended a small-group, 'goal-setting' session (these were usually organized in 'by shift' groups). At this time the observers, aided by the consultants, reminded everyone about the principles of the new approach to safety improvement and how it worked in practice. It was made clear that no individuals could be identified from the observations, and that no disciplinary action would be involved as a result. The actual baseline observations were then announced and the group discussed and agreed on a target for safety improvement that was 'difficult yet achievable'.

The goal-setting sessions followed the 'S.M.A.R.T.' principles of participative goal setting. That is, goals must *specific* and *measurable* – they must be stated in precise terms, for example to increase the percentage of safe behaviours from 55 per cent to 70 per cent, rather than some vague generalizations about 'trying to behave in a more safe way'. They must be *achievable* and *realistic*. The target for improvement should be high enough to be a challenge that is valued by the group and perceived as a worthwhile effort. However, if it is not viewed as 'realistic' the group will become de-motivated and demoralized. Likewise, a target that is regarded as 'too low' will not generate interest or effort. There must be a *time boundary* – a date by which the target should be reached must be agreed, so that the group can work towards the specific goal for safety improvement rather than have some undefined time limit. This means that the feedback charts and graphs can be prepared for the agreed time span, for example 12, 16 or 20 weeks, and thereby act as a continual visual reminder. In this instance the observers were recruited for a total of 20 weeks, namely a 4-week baseline period and a 16-week intervention period. At the end this time they would hand over to newly trained observers for the next phase of the programme.

- The observers then continued their observations and every Friday the results were entered onto the feedback graph. These charts were enlarged to poster size and produced in bright colours (yellow boards with the target line drawn in red) and posted around the plant. (An example is given in Figure 6.2.) Failure to

115

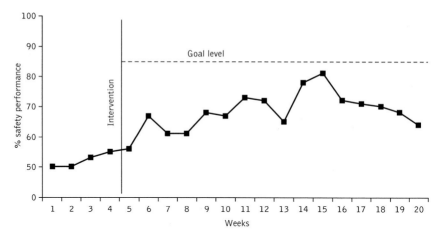

Figure 6.2 *Example of feedback chart*

reach the target was not punished in any way, but instead, feedback and praise were used for what had been achieved. This helped to stimulate discussion on why targets had not been met and what could be done to improve the situation. This observation by peers gains the greatest sense of ownership and involvement, and the feedback reinforces the desired behaviours.

- At the end of end of the first 16-week phase new observers were trained, who then continued observations with a modified checklist. Some behaviours were removed from the checklist, if the observers had continually recorded this as a 'safe behaviour' over a period of time. This meant that additional 'new' items could be added to the checklist. By the end of the eighth phase (i.e. 16-week period) every department had its own checklist of between 6 and 20 items and its own large scoreboard on which the weekly result was displayed together with the target line. (see Figure 6.2). Enlarged copies of the checklist were also displayed near this feedback chart.

Success of the intervention

The majority of employees who took part in this initiative were convinced that it was a success. There was also objective data for this. For example:

- In a typical 16-week period prior to the start of the intervention, the company had 118 accidents, including minor first-aid treatments. A year later there were only 63 similar incidents. Four years later, this figure had fallen to only 26 incidents in the 16-week period (see Figure 6.3).
- In the first two years, three-day lost time accidents (LTAs) fell by 86 per cent and

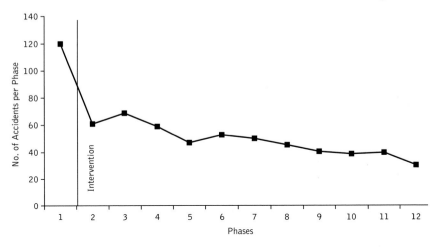

Figure 6.3 *Five-year accident rates*

minor accidents by 72 per cent. The number of LTAs fell from 22 in the year prior to the introduction of the programme to 6 in the following year and to 3 in the year after that.

Not all the improvements observed were quantifiable and the company did acknowledge other benefits. These stemmed mainly from improvements in communication, involvement and commitment. A sense of achievement and pride became manifest as a development in confidence and initiative among the workforce. When the company started preparing its risk assessments it was able to find employees on the shopfloor who were able and willing to do the work. Specialist risk assessment safety committees were now able to carry out assessments for each operation, based on their on-the-job knowledge. Defunct 'hazard' spotting groups came forward and asked to start this activity again. They organized this in their own time and generated their own timetable and programme. A 'suggestion box' was started up again and was actively used.

The 'near-miss' accident reporting scheme was revived with considerable success. Prior to the start of the scheme, management complained that nothing was ever reported, and employees responded by saying that nothing was ever done about any hazards that they did identify: a fairly common impasse in organizations. The increased cooperation led to improved credibility for the scheme. Simple changes led to significant improvements. For example, a report form was produced that had a detachable slip that was returned to the originator to show what action had been taken (what and when, etc.). This was eventually added to the computer system. Now any employee can file 'near miss' reports, suggestions and hazard spotting situations directly at the workstation terminal and gain full access to feedback on the progress of his/her report.

Based on the success of the safety improvement programme we were asked by the management team whether we could apply the same principles to quality improvement. This was an important issue as the company had made the decision to go for a high quality product used in specialist applications. If the high specification was not met the product was virtually useless and could only be sold for such applications as wrapping paper for market stalls. This involved a considerable loss. A sustained high level of quality was, therefore, vital for the continued viability of the plant.

The OBMod continuous quality improvement programme

Based on our experience with the continuous safety improvement programme and taking into account that quality improvement is a more complex process, some modification of the basic model was made and more steps were incorporated into the process. The procedure adopted was as follows:

1   The usual letter of intent was sent to employees from the most senior level of management. This letter included information on why and how the project was taking place, including such information as:
    - a statement about the current situation of the organization and the economic conditions in which it was operating;
    - an explanation of why quality was so important for the company and why continuous quality improvement was necessary (mainly because of the high cost of waste and lost orders due to poor quality);
    - an outline of the advantages for the individual employee (primarily greater job security);
    - a brief description of how the OBMod approach would work in practice;
    - identification of the individuals who would be the champions of the process, or the persons responsible for its implementation, and also an introduction to the external consultants being used (most of whom were already known to most employees from the safety project, but some new members were introduced at this point);
    - an explanation concerning who would be involved (basically everyone eventually, but the letter explained where the scheme would start and how it would expand). This was intended to avoid the problem of any people feeling that they were being singled out for special attention, or alternatively, being left out!
    - An outline of how and when things would happen (i.e an expected timetable of events).
2   A series of semi-structured interviews were carried out with a random sample of personnel. This was to gain an initial feel for attitudes to quality and the quality culture of the organization.
3   The information gathered from the interviews was used to design and pilot a questionnaire for a quality opinion survey, which was then administered to a much

wider sample of the organization. This gave much useful information for the design of the rest of the project, and was fed back to management and was available to everyone. Care was, of course, taken that no individual respondents could be identified in any information circulated. Based on this information it was decided to introduce the concept of internal customers and suppliers (i.e. each department would treat the department preceding it in the flow line as a supplier and the one succeeding it as customer). We also felt that a 'link-pin' structure would be a useful way of looking at the organization (see Box 6.1).

Box 6.1:
LINK-PIN SYSTEM OF ORGANIZATION

Link pin is a system of organization originally suggested by Rensis Likert (1961). On the surface, it involves only a small change from the traditional way that the organizational chart is drawn (see diagram below). However, it represents a considerable difference in the way people relate within the organization. The replacement of lines of authority in the traditional chart by interlinking triangles is to indicate that each group (or department) has the responsibility for setting and achieving its own objectives, in conjunction with other relevant parts of the organization. It is also responsible for signalling to the rest of the system if there are problems in achieving these objectives. This will allow the rest of the system time to adjust to the change in circumstances.

The other difference, which gives the system its name, is that many individuals are members of two or more groups. They become the 'link pins'. The person in the linking position is responsible for ensuring that there is compatibility between the two or more groups of which they are a member. This multiple membership extends in two directions. Links can be up and down, but can also be sideways. Thus, a member of one function (e.g. production), may also be a member of the personnel group. If the system works well, this can solve a problem of traditional organizations – communication and compatibility between functions. Traditionally, any requests for information would have to go up the tree and then down again, with the reply following the same path. The link-pin system allows for quicker and more accurate sideways transfer of information. In traditional organizations, such channels are usually not encouraged. They may develop informally, but if something goes wrong, the 'culprits' are usually instructed to 'follow the correct procedure in future'. The reason for this is that such organizations are built on the premise that authority and responsibility is delegated down the hierarchy. The link-pin system, however, is based upon personal responsibility for the setting and achieving of objectives, and coordinating these with the rest of the organization.

119

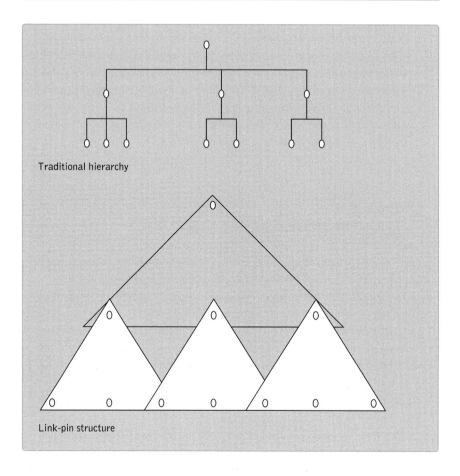

Traditional hierarchy

Link-pin structure

4   In order to better manage this complex process a *Quality Process Steering Group* was established. This was needed since if we were to implement continuous quality improvement in a continuous flow production process there was a need for coordination between departments. In fact existing policies in the plant actually discouraged communication between departments. Workers were disciplined if found outside their own department and thus had virtually no contact with departments above or below them in the production flow. The Steering Group was given appropriate training in the methodology of the intervention, the basic plan of approach and in any necessary management techniques.

5   As a further aid to coordination Departmental Quality Process Improvement Teams were formed. As the name implies there was one for each department and it included members to represent all work teams and shifts. Two of these individuals were also members of the steering group (i.e. to act as the linking pins), and others acted as linking pins to their own internal customer and supplier teams (i.e. across functions or departments) (see Figure 6.4). After training, which

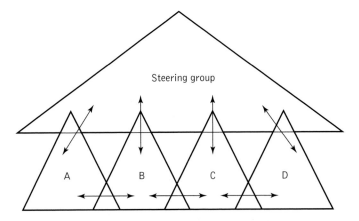

Departmental/function teams A–D

Figure 6.4   *The link-pin organization for the quality intervention*

Notes: The arrows indicate the link-pin function Teams B and C display a full supplier and customer link-pin function

was similar to the design used for the steering group, and which included the development of a team quality policy statement, the critical 'OK quality' behaviour checklist was produced for the department, in agreement with co-workers. Regular meetings of the departmental teams were held to discuss quality behaviour, and to identify the potential barriers to quality performance, both within the department and with internal customer and supplier departments. Problems and issues, which could not be resolved at this departmental level, were passed upwards to be dealt with by the quality improvement steering group. These procedures were designed to aid the application of the behaviour-based approach to the macro issues characteristic of complex organizational change efforts.

6   As indicated above, each departmental process improvement team produced its own critical behaviour checklists. These were written in the same format as for the critical safety behaviour checklists but using the terms 'OK Quality Behaviour' and 'NOT OK Quality Behaviour', rather than 'SAFE' and 'UNSAFE'. Practice sessions using the checklists were held and the final lists were agreed. These were displayed as with the safety checklists.

7   The procedure now continued in the same sequence as that established for the safety improvement programme. That is:

   • A baseline measure for quality performance was established over a minimum period of four weeks.

   • The baseline measure was used to set a target for quality improvement; these were participative goal-setting sessions on exactly the same lines as those for the safety checklists.

121

- The intervention was continued for a period of 12 to 14 weeks; the cycle for this depending on the shift patterns within the department, with the weekly results recorded on a chart within each department.
- Outcomes were discussed by the departmental quality improvement team who modified the process as, and if, necessary. A new cycle of 12 to 14 weeks of observations, with new observers, was then initiated.

Evaluation of the behavioural approach to quality improvement

It is our experience, from this intervention, that defining behaviourally and then positively reinforcing 'OK Quality' behaviour is a viable approach to quality improvement, but it must be supported by a structure and climate which facilitates the changes necessary to sustain a quality culture, such that quality becomes part of 'the way we do things around here'. There is very little doubt that the fact that we had previously carried out a very successful behavioural safety intervention in this same organization contributed to the success of the quality improvement programme. Participants were already very familiar with, and committed to, the behavioural approach. A further effect is that this methodology actually facilitates genuine empowerment. Those taking part had already had experience of taking responsibility for their own behaviour in relation to safety, so that it was relatively easy to extend this to the wider problems of coordination and control involved in quality.

Effect of total intervention

There is no doubt that the combined effect of both the safety and quality change programmes had a marked effect on the overall culture of the organization. The effect was real empowerment. Not the lip service paid to the idea but where very little changes, as so often happens with traditional change programmes. Employees were now taking real responsibility and were anxious to make a contribution. There was considerable evidence for this, in that operators were making suggestions that made a real contribution to performance. These were often the type of thing that the shop floor had probably known about for years but had had no opportunity to get into the system. For example, during production expensive coatings were added. It was also known that the ends of each roll were usually not usable and were cut off and discarded at the end of the production process complete with coatings. The suggestion was made; why not cut them off before coating?

A similar example concerned the treatment of sub-standard production. Workers often knew when a section of a role was not up to standard, but if they pointed this out they received punishment in the form of disapproval from management for poor production. They tended, therefore, to say nothing and the fault was only picked up at the end of the production process, after several additional expensive processes had been carried out. Management changed their approach to rewarding production staff with approval for notifying faults at the earliest opportunity so that these could be identified and the product scrapped without further cost. In another case the effect of the communication engendered by the link-pin system was evident. The production department spent time trying to produce sheet that was completely flat. There was a natural tendency for the edges to be thicker than the centre. It emerged that for the coating department, which came next in the process, it was actually advantageous to have the edges thicker. In other words one department had been trying to produce 'perfect' quality, which was actually making life more difficult for its internal customer.

In psychological terms the intervention had moved the organization from dependence to inter-dependence. This is something that is quite difficult to do. We will explain what we mean by this and what the significance is in the next section.

FROM DEPENDENCE TO INTER-DEPENDENCE

The ideas we wish to develop at this stage centre on the concept of *dependence*, which arises as a reaction to the feeling of being controlled. Whenever authority is being used (as is it very commonly is in most organizations), the individual on the receiving end of this authority is inevitably pushed into a position of dependence. That is to say that because they are always told what to do, and do not have to make decisions for themselves, they eventually become dependent on the authority figure and will not know how to act unless told what to do. Because they have no experience of initiating action, and subsequently being responsible for it, they will be unable to do this, even in situations which, ideally, would require it. Because they have habitually been told what to do, they have become relatively passive during their work life. The longer they have been in this situation the more complete will be their dependence. Most of us do, in fact, get a great deal of experience of dependence. As young children we are dependent on our parents; when very young, literally for our survival. At school, college and early working life, we also spend much of our time in a situation where others make the decisions and we do as we are told. For many people this continues throughout their working lives. In fact, given this background, it is not surprising that we encounter resistance when setting up change programmes, particularly when these involve people taking unaccustomed responsibility. Being suddenly confronted with making decisions and seeing them through in a situation in which one was previously told what to do can be quite frightening. So when resistance is encountered, how does this concept help us to understand and cope with it? To explain this we need to define some other possible relationships, which are connected with authority and dependence. These are shown in Figure 6.5.

Counter-dependence

This arises where the dependent individual wishes to escape from being controlled, but the authority figure will not give up control. In this case, all that the dependent person

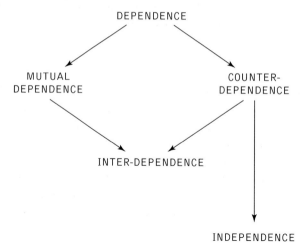

Figure 6.5 *Dependence relationships*

can do is 'fight' back. This will often take the form of some act of rebellion. Whatever the action taken, this is the way it will almost certainly be seen by the authority. 'Wild cat' strikes are good examples of counter-dependence in organizations. Often, the workers concerned feel that this is the only way they can make their feelings known. Strangely enough, a counter-dependent reaction can also arise in, what is, almost the opposite situation, such as when the authority attempts to hand over control before the dependent individual is ready to take responsibility and make their own decisions. In this case the 'fight' is to push the authority back into control. Thus, counter-dependence is really about establishing who is in control and of what.

Mutual dependence

This is a more cooperative situation. Control is shared by mutual agreement, which may, or may not, have been openly negotiated. Usually in organizations the mutually dependent roles have evolved over time, without anyone being too consciously aware of the interrelationship or its implications. However it arises, it always takes the form of each party controlling their own areas of activity, but in a way which is mutually supportive of each other, but neither party takes any responsibility for the other's activities. It is usually quite a powerful relationship, but has the weakness that if one half of the partnership fails in its part, the other half will not pick up their activities. This means that, at best, jobs are left half done or, at worst will cause the collapse of the whole partnership. It is quite a common relationship in the management of professional organizations (accountants managing other accountants or lawyers managing lawyers), where manager and subordinate have equal respect for each other's skills and abilities, and each is confident about their own role, but it does also occur in manufacturing and other types of organization. In mutual dependence both manager and subordinate know their jobs and get on with them, dovetailing together, without the use of authority.

Inter-dependence

Inter-dependence may, on the surface, look rather similar to mutual dependence. The partners may have a tendency to concentrate on their own areas of activity, but they will, if need arises, be capable of taking over each other's roles. Usually, there will be considerable flexibility and interchange of activities. There will be joint decision-making and sharing of control. The relationship will be one of cooperating equals. It is usually a very rewarding and creative way to work, but can be difficult to maintain. Effort and commitment is needed to resolve conflicts and disagreements. In management terms this will be a truly participative system, each partner concentrating on their own job, but able to take over, or assist with, the other's if the occasion demands.

Independence

The final situation to be defined here is not strictly a relationship at all. In the context of this theory independence usually arises from an unsatisfactory resolution of counter dependence, where the conflict is avoided by one party withdrawing from the relationship and proceeding to operate on their own. There is a place for independent working in organizations, but it is obviously better if this is as a result of a conscious decision that this is the best way to work in a particular situation, rather than as a result of an inability to resolve issues of authority and control.

Moving from dependence to inter-dependence

Fairly obviously, the implementation of the behavioural approach to safety (and indeed many other change initiatives) will only be effective in a situation of inter-dependence. If there is a high level of dependence on the part of participants, it will be very hard, if not impossible, to get them to take responsibility for checklists and observations. In fact, getting the balance right is quite difficult. Management must be involved and show interest and support where necessary, but must not take over so that participants lose ownership, or withdraw too far so that participants feel that they have been abandoned and the management are not interested. As indicated above, many organizations have authoritarian cultures, which will have developed relatively high levels of dependence in their employees. This was, after all, the standard for most organizations throughout the nineteenth and the greater part of the twentieth centuries. The issue then is how is it possible to move people from dependence to inter-dependence. Unfortunately, experience teaches us that there is no way to move directly from one to the other. It seems that it is only possible to move via counter-dependence or mutual dependence, or quite often, a combination of both. This is indicated by the arrows in Figure 6.5.

125

Many managers will discover that, if in an attempt to move towards greater participation they give up control too quickly, subordinates move straight into counter-dependence. This will usually involve arguments about who is responsible for the activity or decision involved, with claims that it is the manager's job to take charge. In other cases the response may simply be passive resistance; things simply do not get done. There is evidence that if the person in the authority position persists and refuses to take back control, then eventually the dependent partner(s) will start to assume responsibility. Within organizations this is obviously a fairly dangerous strategy. While the issue of control is being fought out, very little work may be getting done, and the situation can escalate out of control. There is also the danger that if the pressure becomes too much, people will move into independence, either by psychological withdrawal or literally by leaving the organization.

A safer way to move is via mutual dependence. This involves negotiating to hand over control to the subordinate(s) until an equal sharing is achieved. A possible problem with this strategy is that mutual dependence is very comfortable. Because roles are clearly differentiated and work is shared, nobody feels over-controlled or over-responsible. It is also relatively easy to manage because it is clear who is supposed to do what. Consequently, there is a tendency to get stuck in this stage and not make the move on into inter-dependence. In reality, it is very hard to judge the rate at which control can be transferred, so there is always the risk of flipping over into counter-dependence. This means that most change processes will, to some extent, involve both routes: some pressure from management and consequent argument, and some negotiation and smooth transfer of control.

To give a little more insight into this theory it is, perhaps, worth making an aside to point out that what is described above is, in fact, the process of growing up. Following a period of total dependency upon their parents by very young children, the mutual dependence and counter-dependence stages are what are thought of as typical teenage behaviour. Although, in fact, they tend to last from around the age of three or four until the twenties (or in some cases for life). What is going on, of course, is that the child is sorting out who is in control and of what. The wise parent will offer a gradual handover of responsibility but with safeguards ('You can stay out until midnight, if you phone in and let me know where you are'). Being fallible we will not always get it right, and the relationship will tip over into the arguments and tantrums of counter-dependence. If we persevere, the relationship will eventually develop into that of two inter-dependent adults. If not handled properly, the child may retire into independence, either by psychological withdrawal, or more tragically, by simply leaving home and disappearing. It could be argued, by those who are psychoanalytically oriented, that the reason that we have so much trouble with authority at work is because many of us have not fully resolved the problems of dependence which we have with our own parents.

The behavioural approach to resolving dependency

In the early stages of the safety improvement project we did encounter some resistance. This is very normal and took the usual form of doubts expressed about the methodology, initial reluctance to become observers and claims that management were only concerned about production and did not care about safety. There is sometimes a reason for this last perception. Consider the reinforcers for management. If there is pressure on to meet production targets where does the manager's reinforcement come from – meeting the target or enforcing safety regulations? So where do management focus their attention? It is not surprising that in such circumstances they concentrate on meeting targets and so appear fixated on production. To be fair, in our experience most managers do also have a genuine concern for safety.

However, many of the concerns expressed undoubtedly stem from dependence. The initial observers, particularly, tend to feel exposed. They are, after all, being asked to do things and to take responsibility that they have never done before. For this reason, although we call for volunteers some persuasion is often necessary and it is usually safety representatives and others with an interest in safety who are first to respond. We start with a very structured approach, at first very much controlled by the consultants, but gradually we hand over more and more control to the participants until they eventually take complete charge of the process. We thus move from dependence, through mutual dependence, towards inter-dependence. In the case described above we did achieve a relatively high degree of inter-dependence. In other cases where we have simply worked on safety we may only reach a degree of mutual dependence and then only on that particular activity, although in some instances the change in relationship has extended to other areas of operation. The process we are describing here can be expressed in behavioural terms as *contingency contracting*.

Transitional contingency contracting

Contingency contracting is a technique developed by Homme and Tosti (1971), which consists of openly negotiating a contract that specifies both required behaviours and the rewards to be used to reinforce them. *Transitional contingency contracting* is a procedure in which both the specification of required behaviours and control of the system of reinforcement are gradually transferred from the manager to the subordinate(s). It is usually necessary to move through several stages of contingency contracts, starting from a point where the manager has total control of all aspects of the contract and gradually working to a position where control is shared or, if appropriate, to a point where the subordinate is in total control. Homme and Tosti suggested that it is necessary to work through five levels of contracting when working from total dependence to total personal responsibility. Each level may include up to three forms as shown in Table 6.1. Thus in level 1, the manager has control of both the task (desired behaviour) and the reinforcement. In level 2, form 1, the manager still retains control of the task but

Table 6.1   *Five levels of transitional contingency contracting*

Form	Level				
	1	2	3	4	5
1	R–M T–M	R–MS T–M	R–MS T–MS	R–S T–MS	R–S T–S
2		R–M T–MS	R–S T–M	R–MS T–S	
3			R–M T–S		

Notes:
R = Reinforcement
T = Task
M = Manager
S = Subordinate
Source: adapted from Bertold (1982)

negotiates the form of reinforcement with the subordinates. In level 2, form 2, the manager shares control of the task but controls the reinforcement. This procedure continues through the levels as shown, until level 5 is reached, where the subordinate has control of both task and reinforcement.

Transitional contingency contracting is, therefore, a technique for moving, via mutual dependence, from an authority/dependence relationship to one characterized by inter-dependence. The procedure involves a gradual process, negotiated at each stage, for transferring control from manager to subordinate. That the subordinate ends up in control of both tasks and reinforcement may seem to indicate a condition of independence. In some situations this may well be a possibility, but in most cases it will be necessary to regularly coordinate tasks and negotiate how new ones are to be handled. So we would argue that in most organizational contexts the aim of contingency contracting is to achieve inter-dependence.

This may seem an unduly elaborate process, but there is evidence that it is necessary to go through all the stages if the exchange of control is to be carried out smoothly. Berthold (1982), for example, quotes a case where production requirements prompted a manager to move quickly through the sequence, omitting some stages. This created 'total confusion' and a 'growing sense of resentment among workers'. This can be seen as counter-dependence created by too rapid a release of control. Homme and Tosti, in fact, listed ten rules that must be followed if contingency contracting is to be successful:

1   The contract must provide for immediate reinforcement.
2   Initial contracts must call for and reinforce small approximations.
3   Reinforce frequently with small amounts of reward.
4   The contract must call for and reward accomplishment rather than obedience.

5   Reward the performance immediately after it occurs.

6   Include a criterion of quality as well as quantity.

7   The contract must be fair in the sense that the amount of reinforcement and the amount of performance bear a reasonable relationship to each other.

8   The terms of the contract must be clear.

9   The contract must be positive, avoiding the threat of punishment.

10 Contracting as a method must be used systematically.

So far in this chapter we have described a major change intervention which changed the organization concerned from a fairly traditional, moderately authoritarian culture to one where employees experienced a considerable degree of empowerment. After the intervention workers at all levels were more involved with, and able to influence, organizational decisions. This was obviously quite a major culture change. Since this was a case study within one organization we will expand on this and conclude this chapter with a discussion of what is meant by organizational culture and then show how behaviour analysis can be used to give greater insight into this concept. This, in turn, will suggest effective ways of changing culture.

CHANGING ORGANIZATIONAL CULTURE

We will start with some definitions. Although widespread interest in the notion of culture as an important influence on organizational effectiveness is a relatively recent phenomena, probably created by the work of Peters and Waterman (1982), who purported to show that successful companies all shared certain key elements in their culture, the concept has been in use for some time. A relatively early definition, for example, was provided by Eliott Jaques (1951). He defined culture as:

> The customary or traditional ways of doing things, which are shared to a greater or lesser extent by all members of the organization and which new members must learn and at least partially accept in order to be accepted into the service of the firm.

Schein (1984) gives a more complex definition:

> Organizational culture is the pattern of basic assumptions that a given group has invented, discovered or developed in learning to cope with its problems of external adaptation and internal integration, and that have worked well enough to be considered valid, and therefore, to be taught to new members as the correct way to perceive, think and feel in relation to these problems.

Organizational culture is thus the informal and unwritten rules by which people in an organization know how to behave and react, and are what makes such behaviour in one organization different from that in another. This is neatly expressed by James Wilk (1989):

> There may be no formal rules proscribing certain modes of conduct, yet people in the organization quickly learn to follow unwritten rules to the extent that certain patterns of behaviour become ubiquitous in the organization, and, furthermore, serve to mark it out from other organizations, giving it a distinct identity and a distinct flavour or feel. Once you learn the culture of an organization, you know how to conduct yourself wherever you may venture within it.

Wilk then gives the following definition:

> We define the culture of an organization as the invariant patterns of organizational behaviour, considered as a whole, that connect, inform, and provide a context for even the most diverse actions of individual managers right across an organization, that help to distinguish behaviour in that organization from behaviour in others, and are not directly encoded in the organization's formal rules.

It, of course, follows that if the culture is not enshrined in the formal rules of the organization, then it cannot be changed by changing the rules. Culture change is, in fact, very difficult (it has even been argued that it is impossible to do deliberately and in a planned way) and requires time and subtlety of approach.

Traditional methods of culture change

We will consider, briefly, the traditional advice on culture change, in order to provide a comparison with the behavioural approach. A useful outline is provided by Cummings and Huse (1989) as follows:

1 *Clear strategic vision* It is important to start a culture change with a clear view of the direction and purpose of the proposed change. Why is it necessary to change and where is it hoped to end up? Very often this will be enshrined in a company 'mission statement'. This is a statement of the company's goals and how it intends to achieve them. It is important that this should be a clear and precise statement of clear and measurable goals, not just a set of 'motherhood' statements, as is very often the case in practice. The importance of the mission statement, from the point of view of culture, is that it will embody the values which the company leadership espouses, and thus provides purpose and direction for the cultural change.

2 *Top management commitment* It is important that top management are committed to the change, and are seen to be committed. Culture change can really only be managed from the top down. This is because only top management has the power to make changes in the values and deeper structures of the organization.

3 *Symbolic leadership* Senior managers must behave in ways which are consistent with the new culture. More than this, it is necessary to do this with enthusiasm, so that the new culture is communicated through their actions. Hence, also, the need for real internalized commitment at the top.

4 *Supporting organizational changes* It is essential to make changes in the organizational structure, reporting procedures and management styles to bring them into line with the new culture. It is, for example, impossible to move towards a culture embodying participation and empowerment if the organizational systems still require detailed reporting in a strictly hierarchical line system of management. New organizational procedures can also be used to make people aware of the changes that are taking place and encourage the new behaviours that are required.

5 *Change organizational membership* Bringing new members into the organization who already subscribe to the required organizational values and practices is a considerable help to the process of change. By the same token, helping those who do not wish to accept the changes to leave will also speed the process (an activity which Cummings and Huse rather sinisterly refer to as 'termination of deviants').

Changing organizational membership, in this context, does not only mean hiring and firing. It is assumed that it is possible to change, by a number of means, the attitudes and beliefs of individuals who remain within the organization. The most obvious of these is through training and development, but other techniques include formal communication programmes, use of role models who display the required new behaviours (often these are provided by new members hired as part of the change programme), counselling programmes and the participation by organization members in developing the new culture.

It will be noticed that there is a strong similarity in the above methods to the traditional change methods we discussed in Chapter 2, and which we suggested were not very effective. Similar comments apply here. Obviously, these methods will (and do) produce some change, but it might well be more effective to look at culture change from the perspective of behaviour analysis.

Behaviour analysis and culture

In behaviour analysis terms culture can be defined as *that which gets reinforced*. People behave the way that they do because some behaviour pays off and other behaviour does not. It is this selective pattern of reinforcement common to a particular organization which sets up the 'invariant patterns of organizational behaviour' and which Wilk suggests defines organizational culture. We can illustrate this by reference to some specific cultures. We will use a classification suggested by Harrison (1987). This is a little simplistic but provides a description of four different cultures. Most people will have experienced at least one or two of these, some will recognize all four.

Power culture

This type of organization is lead by a strong leader or coalition who run it as if they own it (quite often they do). Decisions are made at the top and are quickly disseminated through the organization. 'Good' employees implement these quickly and efficiently. At its best this type of organization is flexible, reacts quickly to changing circumstances and values creativity and initiative. At worst it is tyrannical and despotic, ruling by fear and punishment.

What gets reinforced

In a power culture this will depend on the boss or top group. If they value initiative and creativity these will be rewarded, either by approval and recognition or pay and promotion (or both), and a creative and dynamic culture will develop. In the more abrasive authoritarian organization reinforcement will be obtained by doing as you are told. Initiative may well attract punishment. The subordinate reinforces the boss by flattery and so stays safe.

Role culture

In this culture power is exercised through rules. It has a clearly defined hierarchy, often with many layers. There will be clearly established procedures and rules for dealing with every eventuality. These will usually be enshrined in large manuals. Think of the classic bureaucracy. A key characteristic is that if you stay within rules you are safe.

What gets reinforced

By and large the level of rewards are low. What reinforcement does occur is for efficient operation of the rules. Innovation tends to be either punished (for breaking the rules) or ignored (extinction). Subordinates reinforce the bureaucrat by conforming (following the rules). We found as academics that we could keep administrative officers happy by doing such things as filling forms efficiently and producing returns on time. This made their lives easier. We were reinforced in return by their cooperation and getting our problems dealt with promptly.

Achievement culture

As its name implies this type of organization is concerned with making a difference in the world, in extreme cases this is done with an almost missionary zeal. Innovation and the development of revolutionary products are valued. The judgement as to whether a development is good and desirable depends on the views of influential members of the organization, not on external or societal values. Hence their efforts to change the world can sometimes go drastically wrong. For instance when Clive Sinclair decided that what the world needed was a small pocket calculator he was proved to be right, as he was again with a small home computer. However, the world decided very conclusively that it did not want a small electric motor car (the C5).

What gets reinforced

Creativity and new ideas are rewarded. Mistakes will not be punished (unless perhaps made too often). In achievement cultures employees are often rewarded by being given time to work on their own pet projects. This provides intrinsic motivation and an opportunity to use the Premack principle. An interesting example of what happens when an organization gets its reinforcement wrong is provided by recent events in university research departments in the UK. Such departments usually espouse an achievement culture and so would be expected to reward innovation and 'good' research. Ideally they should identify the behaviour that produces good research output and then reinforce it. A government initiative, the research selectivity exercise, was designed to improve research by rewarding departments that produced good research results. In many cases it had almost the opposite effect. Departments were assessed on their written research output. Hence much effort went into producing the requisite number of research papers, which reduced time to do research. In fact, at times it produced almost a role culture as people scrambled to produce the requisite number of papers, i.e. attempted to fulfil the rules. In passing, it is worth noting that this initiative also flouted another rule of behaviour modification by rewarding outcomes rather than behaviour (see Chapter 7).

Support culture

Like the achievement culture, this culture is very customer oriented, but instead of using internal reference points, the concern is to find out what the customer wants and then supply this. In the same way there is concern for the welfare of employees oriented towards ensuring that their needs are also met. Warm caring relationships are valued in the organization. Most service organizations aspire to this type of culture.

What gets reinforced

Reinforcement comes from being valued as an individual. If managers show warmth and friendliness to others, this will be reciprocated, so developing a caring environment. There is a danger that people will be reinforced simply for being there, rather than for doing something. Reinforcement will also be received from satisfied customers either simply through verbal interaction or, in some cases, by 'thank you' letters. To give another example from the academic world: it might be expected that a university teaching department would be a support culture, which would enhance mutual learning. To be fair most such departments do have strong elements of such a culture. However, with increasing legalism and promulgation of rules and regulations for both staff and students, reinforcement is increasingly centring on the provision of specific information to students on course requirements and correct completion of various bureaucratic returns. This produces a high element of role culture, which is not the best way of fostering learning.

It will be apparent from much of the above that one problem with attempting to understand the culture of an organization is that there is often a mismatch between what management say about the culture and what actually happens. This is an example of a phenomenon that Argyris (1962) noticed to be common in many aspects of management. He pointed out that there is often a difference between the *espoused theory* (what managers say they believe) and the *theory in use* (what managers actually do). This discrepancy does not only occur in management, it can be found in all aspects of life. Some of our own students have on occasion even had the temerity to suggest that our own espoused theories of teaching do not always match how we actually teach. The espoused theory is what you will get if you ask managers what they do. You can only get to the theory in use by observing what people actually do. In the same way the responses obtained by asking people about the culture of their organization will be heavily biased by espoused theories. To find the underlying culture it is necessary to observe what people actually do and then ask the question: 'what is reinforcing this behaviour'.

Changing culture

To change the culture of an organization using the behavioural approach is essentially similar to that used for any other behaviour change, but more complicated. Instead of the traditional process involving a mission statement, which most employees will regard with considerable scepticism, particularly if they enshrine values which are very different from those existing at the present, followed by various training initiatives think in terms of the following steps.

- Remember that culture change is a long and complicated process and will take time.
- It is, therefore, best done in a series of steps or stages, gradually moving from the existing culture to the new (the process of shaping).
- Define the behaviour which will characterize the culture you are trying to create.
- How can the new behaviour be reinforced?
- What existing behaviour needs to change?
- What reinforcement is keeping this going and how does this need to be changed?
- Identify the best place to start – which section or department is likely to respond best to the planned changes? This could be the one which is most enthusiastic, or the one where least change is needed. It is obviously desirable to start with a success.
- Determine how best to extend the project through the organization. In what sequence will departments become involved?
- Remember that the whole project will be much more likely to succeed if employees are involved at all stages. They should participate in defining the

behaviours and in the methods of reinforcement. This will involve some training in the theory and techniques of the behavioural approach.

- Finally, be prepared for the project to evolve and change as time goes on. This will be particularly so, as more people become involved and make contributions.

In the next, and final, chapter we explain some of the more technical issues involved in the application of the behavioural approach and discuss some of the practical problems involved.

CHAPTER SUMMARY

In this chapter we have shown how the behavioural approach can be used to manage on an organization-wide basis. By their very nature these techniques are, of course particularly relevant to organizational change. The basic principles involved are the same as for all other applications of behaviour modification, that is, define the behaviour you wish to develop and any behaviour you want to discourage and find ways to reinforce the new behaviours and extinguish the old. The main difference when carrying out organizational change, rather than individual, is the need to influence large numbers of individuals at one time. Reinforcement is, therefore, usually given on a group basis via feedback charts. We have described how this approach was used in a major change intervention in one organization involving both safety and quality improvement. At the end of the chapter we have also given a more generalized account of how these principles apply to culture change.

In any change process there is always the possibility of resistance from those involved. It is important to listen to what people are saying about why they are unhappy with the change – they may have a valid point, which needs consideration. The best way to avoid unnecessary resistance is to proceed openly and participatively, in this way problems will be raised early in the process and can be resolved. One key issue, which may generate resistance and make participation difficult, is the necessity for a shift from dependence to inter-dependence. This needs to be done in small planned stages possibly using the framework provided by transitional contingency contracting.

Chapter 7

Applying the behavioural approach

The present chapter will deal with some techniques that will be important for successful implementation of a behaviour change programme.

We have previously mentioned that Luthans and Kreitner (1985) have suggested that any change programme needs to follow the five steps below:

1 identify the behaviour;
2 measure the behaviour;
3 functionally analyse the behaviour, i.e. identify the consequences and antecedents of both the desirable and undesirable behaviours;
4 intervene to change the behaviour;
5 evaluate to determine whether or not behaviour and performance have changed in the desired direction.

So far this book has concentrated on the third of these, the consequences and antecedents. What is also required is to identify and measure the behaviour it is hoped to change. This is fairly simple, but there are some traps into which the unwary may fall and this chapter will describe how behaviours can be correctly identified and measured.

Before reading further, try the following exercise:

You are an advanced driving instructor. You have been asked by a friend, who passed their driving test some years ago, to sit with them and see if you consider them to be a 'safe' driver. Produce a list of about ten things that you will be looking for when you go on the drive with your friend.

SPECIFYING BEHAVIOUR

We continually give, and are given, advice on how to behave.

'Take care' (sign beside the escalators in a large department store)

'Please drive safely' (roadside sign on entering a small village)

'Adhere to a reasonable dress code' (sign in the Common Room of the Manchester School of Management)

'Show more initiative' (comment by a boss on a manager's annual appraisal report)

'Keep your bedroom tidy' (injunction delivered at some time by all parents to their children).

The list is potentially endless. We also give advice to ourselves.

'I must use my time more effectively.'

'I must communicate more.'

'I must pay more attention to the needs of my subordinates.'

All of the advice given above is, no doubt, well meant. The problem is that the behaviour required to achieve these desirable goals is not made clear. What does one have to *do* to 'take care', 'drive safely', 'show more initiative', or 'use my time more effectively'?

Precisely specifying behaviour is the first step in trying to change it. Without a good behaviour specification, any behavioural change project is doomed. Although this may appear easy, this is often the point at which basic mistakes are made. Once the principles are grasped, however, specifying what is required in precise behavioural terms becomes a relatively straightforward task.

(*Note*: In the examples that follow the emphasis will be on specifying desirable behaviour that you want to occur. The reason for this is that, in general, it is easier to work on increasing the desirable rather than decreasing the undesirable. There are, however, some circumstances where reduction of the undesirable is the prime focus, e.g. cutting down on smoking, or snacking between meals. The principles of behaviour specification that will be described apply to whether it is desired to increase or reduce the behaviour concerned.)

Let us now return to your safe-driving items and use these as examples. The results from this exercise inevitably vary, but some of the most common items are:

- correct use of rear-view mirror
- observes speed limit
- correct tyre pressures
- indicates properly when manoeuvring
- keeps up with traffic
- being aware of road conditions
- having a valid driving licence
- does not drive too close to the vehicle in front
- observes road signs
- consideration to other road users.

All of these are, of course, what would be expected of a safe driver. (There may occasionally be some conflict between some of the items, for example 'observing the speed limit', and 'keeping up with the traffic', which will have to be resolved.)

The problem with most of these items can perhaps be best demonstrated by imagining a possible disagreement between the driver and instructor. You, as the instructor, tell your friend that they drive too close to the vehicle in front. Your friend hotly disputes this. How can the argument be resolved? (Contrast this with a disagreement as to whether the driver exceeds the speed limit. This disagreement can easily be resolved by looking at the speedometer.)

What is required to resolve the disagreement (and possibly save the friendship) is a precise specification of what constitutes 'too close'. One way of doing this is the 'two second rule'. When the vehicle in front passes a fixed marker, e.g. a particular lamp-post, a least two seconds must pass before your vehicle passes the same point. Counting two seconds is relatively easy. For example, saying 'only a fool breaks the two second rule' at a normal rate of speech takes approximately two seconds. (Using this method has the additional advantage that it automatically takes into account the speed of the vehicle.)

In psychological terminology what is required of a good description of a behaviour is that it has high 'inter-rater reliability'. In other words two people, observing the same behaviour, would agree almost 100 per cent of the time as to whether the behaviour was occurring or not.

Some of the items given above obviously fulfil this criterion better than others. We have already mentioned observing the speed limit. Other items that fulfil the conditions are 'correct tyre pressures', and 'holding a valid driving licence'. Both of these can be checked in ways that would normally lead to the resolving of any disagreement. But consider 'correct use of rear-view mirror'. How might this be specified in ways that would resolve potential disagreements? (Have a go at specifying this behaviour before reading further.)

There are a number of ways in which this behaviour can be specified. One common specification, for example, is 'looks in rear view mirror at least once every x seconds'. Sometimes instructors cover up the rear-view mirror at random intervals and ask the driver to describe the vehicle behind. This may also give some indication of the extent to which the driver is aware of surrounding traffic conditions. Whatever the description chosen, however, the behaviour must fulfil the requirements of being *specific*, *observable* and *measurable*.

The last of these, being measurable, is a further check on whether the behaviour has been properly specified. *If an objective measure of incidence of the behaviour cannot be produced it is likely that it has not been specified precisely enough.* (We will deal later on with the different types of measures that can be used.)

Getting the right behaviour

Making sure that it is the right behaviour that gets rewarded, and the wrong behaviour that gets punished, may appear to be obvious. It is not uncommon, however, for organizations inadvertently to punish the behaviour that they wish to encourage, and vice versa. One common example is the allocation of annual budgets within organizations. Most organizations urge all their departments to be as efficient as possible and to save money. If, at the end of the financial year, an efficient department has heeded this advice and is under-spent on its budget, what happens? In our experience the surplus is often 'clawed back' by the financial administrators and the following year's budget is cut. The department has been punished for doing precisely what was asked of it!

Before going further you might like to try the following case study.

Case study:
BAGGAGE HANDLERS

You are the customer complaints manager for a large charter airline and you have recently been receiving a lot of complaints from customers concerning baggage handling at your local airport. The largest number of complaints concern the amount of time passengers have to wait for their luggage after disembarking.

The baggage handling is carried out by a private contractor. You are aware that this contract, as with those with other private contractors, will contain service targets. If these targets are not met there are penalty clauses that take effect. In addition, if the company consistently fails to meet the targets the airline is likely to review the contract and possibly move it to another contractor.

You have contacted the person in your organization responsible for monitoring the contract and there does not appear to be a problem with the contractor meeting the targets. Before checking the details of the targets written into the contract you decide to go to the airport and observe what is happening in the baggage collection area.

Your observations in the baggage area quickly reveal a common pattern. There are three baggage carousels and the problem occurs when all three are in use, i.e. at periods when a number of planes are arriving within a short time. Once the passengers begin to arrive in the baggage collection area it is only a few minutes before the first bags appear on the carousel. After about 20 bags have appeared, however, the flow stops and it can be 30 or 40 minutes before the rest of the luggage appears.

What do you think is happening, and why? In particular, what do you expect to find when you examine the service targets in the contract?

Analysis

There is an old management saying, which has some truth to it, that 'what gets measured gets managed'. It is likely that, in this case, the baggage handlers have worked out what is being measured and, perhaps more importantly, what is not, and adjusted their behaviour accordingly.

Although we have not had access to the contract, the behaviour of the handlers suggests that the service targets are not specified fully enough. It is likely that there is a maximum time specified between the arrival of the aircraft and the arrival of the first bags on the carousel. It is unlikely, judged by the handlers' behaviour, that there is any target for the arrival of the *last* bag. When under pressure, therefore, the handlers achieve their target by putting a few bags from each flight on the relevant carousel. Once they have done this they can move on to the next flight, returning to the original flight only once they have achieved the targets for the other flights.

Another example of inappropriate targets can be found in the behaviour of a train operating company in the south of England. The performance targets specified that the trains arrive at the terminus within a certain 'window' of its scheduled time. Any lateness beyond this attracted a financial penalty. The company's response to this was somewhat bizarre. If a train was running so late that it would attract penalties, the driver was instructed not to stop at any more stations! Lateness was penalized, not stopping at stations was not. (The company has since lost the franchise. Hopefully the targets have been revised.)

Getting the right behaviour correctly specified in behavioural terms may, by itself, bring improvements in performance. It is often assumed that staff will know what is expected of them, but this is not necessarily the case. Anderson *et al.* (1988) used behavioural techniques to improve the effectiveness of cleaners working in a bar. They developed behavioural items that were then made known to the cleaners. Before the behavioural intervention was introduced efficiency improved by 13 per cent. This improvement in efficiency that is achieved by behavioural specification alone is known as the *clarification effect*. You may recall from Chapter 1 the example of the student working in a bar who tripled her levels of tips by adopting simple changes to her own behaviour. We will deal with another example of where clarification of required behaviour might help improve efficiency later in this chapter.

Behaviour *not* outcomes

One of the ways used in organizations to try and ensure that the correct behaviour is encouraged is to reward the *outcomes* of behaviour, rather than the behaviour itself. This distinction may appear minor but is, in fact, often crucial. Let us look at some examples where the rewarding of certain outcomes can produce counter-productive results.

Organizations, quite laudably, like to have a good accident record. It might appear natural, therefore, to reward staff for having low levels of accidents and near-misses. On reflection, however, this may produce unexpected results. If people are rewarded for not having accidents and/or near-misses, then it is in their interest to 'cover-up' such events. Whilst this may, in the short term, make the figures look good, it may have the effect of storing up a future disaster. Almost every inquiry into a major disaster has found that the events that culminated in the accident had occurred before. On these occasions, however, disaster had been avoided, but no remedial action taken. What is required are not schemes that tend to suppress the reporting of near-misses, but schemes that encourage their reporting, so that action may be taken. What should be rewarded is *safe behaviour*. If people *behave* safely, this will inevitably lead to a good accident record.

Another example comes from personal experience. One of the authors, at one point in his career, worked for an organization with a high-powered, and very well rewarded, salesforce. In order to encourage sales the company ran frequent competitions, based on sales figures. These were generally competitive, with the highest rewards going to the best performing salesperson.

It became apparent to the author, however, that this encouraged behaviour in the salesforce that was not always in the organization's best interests. Often sales staff would receive sales leads that they could not follow up, as they were on the 'patch' of another member of staff. Rather than passing these leads they kept them to themselves. Passing them on might mean that your colleague beat you to the prize. Contrast this with a system that rewards sales staff for carrying out the *behaviours* that, if undertaken, should lead to increased sales.

A programme that followed this technique was carried out in an American estate brokerage firm (Hall, 1983). Although it was the largest in the region in terms of staff, it was only seventh out of 15 in sales. The company employed 27 full-time, and 8 part-time agents, almost equally divided between male and female. After analysing the behaviours that led to successful sales it was decided to target the first two behaviours in the chain that leads to sales;

the number of *initial*, face-to-face, customer contacts, and

the number of *follow-up*, face-to-face, customer contacts.

The number of such contacts was self-reported by agents, but a check was kept by telephone calls and 'courtesy cards'. These cards were sent to contacts, asking the potential customer for comments on the agent's visit. Each week an agent had to report at least 6 initial and 15 follow-up calls. For calls beyond this minimum tokens were awarded which could be exchanged for any of 60 items. These ranged from ten gallons of petrol (11 points), to a slate pool table (1,000 points). The cost to the company of each token was 35 cents. Tokens were dispensed at biweekly sales meetings.

(Although, at the moment, we are only considering the correct choice of behaviour, it is perhaps worth noting the results of the programme. In the year before the programme the firm employed 8 per cent of agents in the area and had 6 per cent of the local market. During the year in which the programme was running these figures were 5 per cent and 12 per cent respectively. In addition attendance at sales meetings rose from an average of 50 per cent to 97 per cent. If the right behaviour is encouraged, results will naturally follow.)

One of the advantages of rewarding behaviour rather than outcomes in this case is that it is often seen as fairer by those involved. Although organizations try to make sales areas as similar as possible this is rarely achievable in practice. A salesperson may do everything right and yet, despite their best efforts, not achieve the sales required. Concentrating on the behaviours helps avoid this. Often, therefore, it is better to use behaviours rather than outcomes when there are uncontrollable factors between the behaviour and outcome.

The rule about specifying the behaviour that leads to outcomes rather than goals was neatly exemplified in the project of a part-time student who was trying to increase the number of goals he scored (no pun intended). The student was a professional ice hockey player, doing a part-time MBA. Although he was primarily a defender, scoring a few goals each season would demonstrate a degree of versatility and hence increase his potential income and transfer value. His objective, therefore, was to increase the number of goals he scored. As a defender, the occasions on which he was in a position from which a shot at goal was realistic were fairly few. He realized, however, that when these occasions arose he was not taking full advantage of them. As all his games were recorded on video for coaching purposes, he analysed them to see why he was not scoring more often. He found that, when he was in a position to shoot at goal, he took the shot very quickly without first looking up to check the precise position of the goal. The behaviour that he decided to work on, therefore, was looking at the goal before taking the shot.

This example demonstrates another reason for working on behaviour rather than outcomes. Often the outcomes occur infrequently – too infrequently for behavioural change techniques to be very effective. Behaviour, on the other hand, can be rewarded much more quickly.

A final example will indicate how concentrating on outcomes, rather than the behaviour that will produce the outcomes, may often be less than effective. In this case a manager decided that he wanted to keep his desk tidy. He quite rightly decided that he needed an 'objective' measure of tidiness so that he could evaluate the effectives of his intervention. He therefore produced a number of measures such as the percentage of desk covered by papers, the height of piles of papers, etc. Despite having a mass of data as to how tidy his desk was at different times of the day he was disappointed to find that his desk was not getting any tidier. He realized that he had, in effect, been concentrating on measuring the outcomes rather than the behaviour. His problem was soon solved when he changed his target to 'the filing and storage within five minutes of receipt of all material unrelated to the task in hand'. This behaviour produced the desired outcomes.

Complex behaviours

In the examples given above, and others we will use, the behaviour concerned is relatively simple to describe. Some, however, like 'driving well' or 'behaving safely' are too complex to be directly observable. This is because they are not themselves behaviours – they are generalizations derived from the observation of a large number of behaviours. The precise behaviours that lead to these generalizations will need to be specified.

This specification is, in fact, what you attempted to do if you did the exercise at the beginning of the chapter. A similar process will have to be done with, for example, 'behaving safely', which is comprised of many separate 'safe' behaviours.

(Before going further it might be worth making a general point about behavioural descriptions. Using descriptions that involve 'not doing something' should be avoided. Behaviour that does not occur is difficult to see. If, for example, you specify the behaviour as 'not contributing in meetings' it will be difficult for someone else to know when this is happening. Is the person concerned quiet because they feel they have nothing that they could usefully contribute, or because they feel inhibited through a lack of self-confidence? The general rule, even when it is your own behaviour that you are trying to change, is that the behaviour should be capable of being observed by a third party.)

The following are some of the behaviours used to encourage workers in a paper mill to behave safely.

- safety footwear to be worn at all times
- hard hats/bump caps to be worn in designated areas
- ear protection to be worn in designated areas
- eye protection to be worn when handling solvents
- mask and gauntlets to be worn when handling caustic
- gloves to be worn when handling waste
- gloves to be worn when pushing reels.

Two points need be made: one about the nature of the items on the list, the other concerning how the items are generated. First notice that all the items are phrased positively. The emphasis, as in most behavioural projects, is the encouragement of the positive, rather than punishment of the negative. The items should reflect this. The second point concerns *who is responsible* for generating the items. In the case of safety, as with many other aspects of jobs, including quality, the people who are actually doing the job usually know more about it than anyone else. It is desirable, therefore, that the prime responsibility for the generation of items should lie with them. There is another good reason why this should be so. In general people feel more committed to changes about which they have been actively consulted. (For a more detailed description of how to design and implement a behaviourally based safety programme, see Sutherland *et al.*, 2000.)

Having specified the behaviour the next step is to measure how frequently it is occurring, before any attempt is made to change it. This is known as developing a *baseline*.

How to measure behaviour

Once the behaviour has been specified, it is essential that a fairly accurate record should be kept of the baseline level of behaviour. As we saw in Chapter 1, just measuring the behaviour may lead to improvements in effectiveness through the clarification effect. Also, as Luthans and Kreitner (1985) have pointed out, 'It is interesting that this measurement step itself may become an intervention (that is, cause the behaviour to change because it is now being measured), and, if it does have the desired impact on performance, this is fine'. The question remains, however, as to what should be measured, and how.

There are two main ways in which behaviour can be measured – frequency and time. You can, for example, measure the number of times the behaviour occurs – this would be a measure of its frequency of occurrence. On the other hand you may not be interested in how often a behaviour occurs but how long it lasts – this would involve a time-based measure. Perhaps the best way of illustrating the difference between the two types of measurement and how they are used in practice is to give some examples.

Example: the 'inefficient' clerk

The clerk concerned had recently been employed in a small section of a utilities company. The section's main, and most important, function was to respond to emergency telephone calls. The job was that of a general administrative assistant, but a critical feature of the job was to answer incoming phone-calls as quickly as possible, in case there was an emergency to be dealt with. If the clerk did not answer the telephone after six rings the system automatically activated a buzzer. If this happened, it was the responsibility of the person nearest the phone to answer it.

The manager of the section thought that the buzzer seemed to be sounding more than had been the case in the immediate past. She did not know, however, if this was due to an increased number of calls or some other factor. In order to establish a baseline, she moved her seating position so that she could see and hear the telephone when it rang.

She then monitored the frequency of what happened using a simple form in which she put a tick each time the phone rang and a tick each time the buzzer operated. The form is shown in Figure 7.1. As can be seen she monitored the behaviour each day for a week.

In passing, it is also worth noting that she recorded what the clerk was doing when the buzzer sounded. She collected this data in order to carry out a Premack analysis. As can be seen the clerk was not 'slacking', she was carrying out other duties. This may suggest that answering the phone is, for some reason, low on her Premack hierarchy.

This example uses a measure of the *frequency* of the behaviour. In other words *how often* the behaviour occurs over a particular period of time. This is sometimes referred to, for obvious reasons, as *event recording*.

Although frequency measures are perhaps the most common form of measurement, it may, on occasion, be more appropriate to use a measure of the behaviour which is based on time, rather than on event. There are two main 'time-based' measures – duration and latency.

Duration is, as its name suggests, a measure of how long a behaviour lasts. For example, if the objective is to increase the contributions an employee makes in meetings, a measure of how *many* contributions (frequency) are made may not tell the whole story.

144

Employee: Administration clerk

Behaviour: Allowing telephone to activate buzzer

Day	Total number of calls	Times buzzer activated	Activity when buzzer activated
Monday	25	15	Faxing (3), delivering mail (2), in kitchen (5), photocopying (5)
Tuesday	27	13	Delivering mail (2), in kitchen (3), photocopying (5), shredding (2), typing (1)
Wednesday	18	9	Faxing (2), in kitchen (2), typing (2), photocopying (3)
Thursday	17	8	Delivering mail (1), in kitchen (2), typing (3), photocopying (2)
Friday	17	6	Faxing (2), delivering mail (1), photocopying (2), tidying stationery cupboard (1)
Total	104	51	Percentage occurrence 49 per cent

Figure 7.1 *Behaviour recording form*

It may be, for example, that the employee makes five 'contributions' during the course of a meeting, but that these are merely 'yes' or 'no' responses to questions. Of more interest may be the duration of these contributions, i.e. the total length of time during which the individual was contributing. Duration will, in these circumstances, be a better measure. The degree of accuracy required will determine how the duration is measured. It may, for example, be possible to measure the length of time the behaviour occurs with a stopwatch. More commonly, however, it will be sufficient to use a tick-list in, for example, five-minute 'blocks'. You may recall the example of the student working in a drug store that was used to introduce the Premack principle in Chapter 3. She used such five-minute 'blocks' to record how long it took her fellow workers to complete each task.

Duration concentrates on how long a behaviour lasts. Latency, on the other hand, is a measure of the *delay* between when a behaviour should occur and when it actually occurs. Again an example will, we hope, make this clear.

Example: the sleepy manager

The problem this manager had was getting up in the morning. Although she set her alarm radio for the correct time she did not get up straight away. She decided, therefore, to measure the time between the alarm radio switching itself on, and the time she actually got up. This is a measure of latency – the time between when the behaviour of getting out of bed *should* occur and when it actually occurred.

Although we are primarily concerned with the measurement of the baseline, it may be of interest to consider her findings, and the solution to her problem.

Over a period of four weeks she found that, on average, there was a delay (latency) of 18 minutes between the alarm radio switching on and her getting out of bed. She also noted that her alarm was tuned to her favourite radio station. Her solution was simple: she tuned her alarm radio to a station she hated and placed it on the far side of the bedroom so that she had to get out of bed to switch it off. (The 'getting out of bed' behaviour was negatively reinforced. As a result of getting out of bed the nastiness stopped.) The plot of the baseline and the effects of the intervention are shown in Figure 7.2.

Another example of the use of when a latency measure is appropriate is the visit report case study in Chapter 4. You may recall that the manager concerned was not filling in his visit reports within a day of the visit, as was expected. The measure he used was the delay, in days, between the visit and the report writing.

Although time-based measures are not used as often as frequency-based measures, they are sometimes more appropriate. In particular, latency is often the most appropriate measure for problems involving procrastination.

Finally, it is often the case that more than one measurement may be used. If you are trying to increase your use of a gym, for example, it may well be worth recording not only the frequency of visits, but also their duration.

Measuring behaviour that cannot be observed all the time

When you are measuring the behaviour of yourself it is possible to record every instance of a behaviour. Sometimes, however, this is not possible. If you are recording the

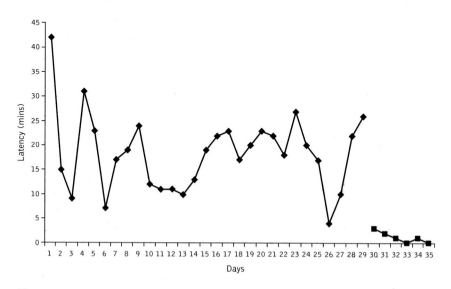

Figure 7.2 *Getting out of bed*

behaviour of others it may not be practical to observe them all the time, especially if there are large numbers of people involved, possibly spread over a large area. Consider the example of the encouragement of the use of ear defenders in a factory, where there may be dozens of individuals, spread over a large area.

In these cases a common solution is to 'sample' the behaviour over a reasonable period of time. In the safety example, observers who are measuring the baseline are asked to make two observations per day of the area for which they are responsible. These observations are carried out at random. Over a period of a week the random samples can be combined to produce a fairly accurate assessment of the actual occurrence of the behaviour. By taking random 'snapshots' a reasonably accurate picture can be generated.

As has been mentioned, the precise specification of behaviour in a *precise, observable* and *measurable* form is a fundamental requirement for any behavioural change project. There are, however, other benefits that may flow from this process, demonstrated by the example of the clerk who failed to answer the emergency telephone. For the first time a manager can get an accurate indication of the scale of the 'problem'. Dealing with all problems involves cost, if only the manager's time. This cost has to be set against the expected benefits if the problem is resolved. It is not unusual to find that managers do not have an accurate perception of the scale of some problems. In the example of the clerk the manager was surprised at the percentage of calls that went unanswered and decided to take action. The opposite can also occur. When the scale of the problem is accurately assessed it may become apparent that the problem was not as large as had been thought. In these cases it may sometimes be decided to live with a problem that would cost too much to put right.

In the case of the clerk the manager was surprised to find that her data showed that the clerk was failing to answer almost half of incoming calls. Thus it became clear to her that what she thought *might* have been a problem was indeed a problem. (The baseline also, of course, provides the data for assessing the efficacy of any intervention to deal with the problem.)

Having successfully specified the behaviour/s that you want to change it is then necessary to consider the consequences that are influencing the behaviour.

RESISTANCE TO CHANGE

This book is about change and so it is appropriate to end with some discussion of the issues that may arise during this process and particularly at the problem of resistance. It should be said first that there is a widespread myth that people inevitably dislike change and will always do their best to avoid it. While it may be true that change programmes do on occasion provoke resistance, this is by no means a universal reaction. Indeed, on many occasions people enjoy change and look forward to it. If this were not so, the rapid rate of change we have seen in the world over the last 20 or 30 years would not have taken place. Most of this change has occurred because people voluntarily and enthusiastically adopted new technologies. This is, of course, because it was seen to make life better (by those who adopted it anyway). Change that is resisted is that which is seen to make life more difficult. However, almost all change, except the most trivial, does require some effort of adjustment, so it is worth looking at what may be happening during this process.

Stages of adjustment

There are a number of theories which suggest that an individual has to work through a series of stages in the process of adjusting to a major change in behaviour or circumstances. The stages are the same however the change is brought about: whether self-initiated or imposed from without. Most of these theories originate from clinical psychology and are concerned with major life changes but are also applicable to the usually less dramatic changes in organizational life. In our work with managers we have found the theory developed by Hopson (Cooper and Makin, 1984), which is based upon Kubler-Ross (1969), to be particularly useful. While there is little empirical evidence to support stage theories we have found them to be useful in helping people to understand and cope with change.

Hopson's model is illustrated in Figure 7.3. It will immediately be noticed that there are no numerical scales attached to either of the dimensions. The horizontal dimension of time, for example, has no specific time periods marked. This is deliberate, because although people may go through the same process in adapting to change, they do so at different rates and with different intensities. We will start with a brief description of each of the stages.

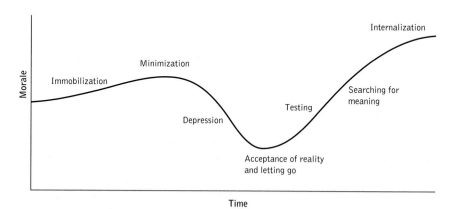

Figure 7.3 Stages of adjustment

Immobilization

The basic problem of adapting to change is that of maintaining some stability whilst achieving the change. If the rate of change is not too fast, people do not have great problems in adapting. Change becomes a process of gradual evolution. If the change is dramatic and/or fast, the normal processes of adaptation may, for a short time, be overwhelmed. The initial reaction of many people when faced with such dramatic changes is to 'freeze up', rather like a rabbit caught in a headlight beam. The freezing is, however, largely cognitive. Behaviourally, the individual in this stage will still continue to function but may appear to be on 'auto-pilot'. Many surrounding cues may be generally unchanged and continue to initiate routine behaviours. The individual may thus respond by carrying out routine tasks, apparently not having recognized or taken in the fact that circumstances have changed. The length and severity of this reaction depends upon such factors as the size of change and the person's ability to cope.

Minimization

The immobilization stage is, by its very nature, a *passive* stage. The minimization stage, on the other hand, is an *active* stage, although at times this may not be apparent. Whilst recognizing that change has occurred, the person minimizes the importance of the change. Cues that minimization may be taking place are statements such as 'It's not really going to make that much difference', or 'really it is just a minor reorganization' when objectively quite a big change is going on. Periods of minimization or denial alternate with bursts of recurrent concerns about the change. This is evidence that the stage is active rather than passive. The individual is actively trying to cope with the change, albeit it in small 'chunks'. The data from experience is being processed and gradually internalized. Both the immobilization and minimization stages were previously seen as undesirable and dysfunctional. It is now generally accepted that they are necessary stages in the adaptation to change. However, they may become dysfunctional if their length or depth become excessive.

Depression

Most people are familiar with the characteristics of depression. The depressed individual lacks motivation, is lethargic, and their mood is generally negative. This is a not uncommon state during periods of major change. In organizations the most usual manifestation is that people feel 'fed-up', show low involvement, and morale is generally low. It may appear to be dysfunctional and may well be so if it lasts for too long a time, but it is a sign that the individual is beginning to accept that the change has occurred. So, on the positive side, it should be seen as the start of the process of adjustment.

Letting go

At this stage the individual has come to accept the reality and permanence of the change, and begun to accept this new reality. This acceptance also leads to a 'letting go' of the past and a beginning to prepare for the future. People start to feel more positive. The attitude becomes 'OK it has happened we might as well make the best of it'.

Testing

Although the individual may have let go of the old reality they may well not have a clear idea (or indeed any idea) of how to behave in the future. There is, therefore, a process of testing out new possibilities. This may either be by actually trying out new behaviours, or by imagining what the new behaviours might be like. The testing stage is one in which there is increasing energy and motivation. The individual is keen to develop and try out new skills and behaviours.

Searching for meaning

Eventually, following the activity of the testing stage, the individual finds time in which to reflect on the changes that have taken place and their own reactions to that change. Positively, the search for meaning concentrates on unforeseen, but positive outcomes. If all goes well this can lead to individuals feeling that they are more effective and 'in charge' as a result of their experience. They begin to have the feeling that life is not so bad after all.

Internalization

In the internalization stage the new thoughts, feelings and behaviour become stabilized as part of the normal functioning of the individual.

Whilst we have tended to concentrate on the effects of changes that are perceived as negative the model also, according to Hopson, has application to positive changes, which are welcomed by the individual. These still require adjustment. Examples from everyday life, which illustrate this, are such happy events as marriage or the arrival of a baby which have been known to produce a similar sequence of events as that described by the model. We have to adjust to both positive and negative change.

Understanding the stages

We can now interpret each of the stages in Hopson's model from the perspective of the behavioural approach.

The length and severity of the *immobilization* stage will be determined, to a large extent, by the threat the change in question is perceived as presenting. Whether the change is perceived as threatening will depend upon the individual's assessment of the threat, and their perceived ability to cope. In terms of Bandura's (1982) social cognitive theory, this latter assessment is related to the individual's assessment of *self-efficacy*. If the individual feels competent in their ability to cope, the immobilization phase may be very short. Obviously, therefore, change may be seen as more or less threatening, but the question arises as to why such threat should lead to denial and minimization? This reaction is entirely understandable in terms of reinforcement. Threats are unpleasant. Any strategy that removes this unpleasantness will, therefore, be negatively reinforcing. (Remember that negative reinforcement leads to an increase in any behaviour that removes an unpleasant stimulus.) Denial removes the anxiety and hence will be likely to occur again. This removal of anxiety by the process of denial may also explain the bursts of apparent euphoria that often occur in this stage. Activity also has the effect of reducing anxiety. The activity of resisting any reduction in one's area of control is, therefore, also negatively reinforcing.

The stage of *depression* has a number of interpretations. Perhaps one of the most useful relates to Seligman's (1975) concept of *learned helplessness* (see Chapter 4). A feature of this syndrome is the persistence of 'fixated behaviour patterns'. These consist of patterns of behaviour that have, in the past, been effective but are now inappropriate. Despite its inappropriateness, at least as perceived by bystanders, the behaviour continues. Many managers will be familiar with this situation. Individuals continue to operate old systems, even though new systems have taken over. Often employees will insist on maintaining the old, even whilst operating the new. This pattern of learned helplessness and fixated behaviour, has considerable similarities with reactive depression. (Note that this explanation is only for depression brought on by particular events. There are other types of depression for which a behavioural explanation may be inappropriate.) In behavioural terms, things that were reinforcers before the onset of the reactive depression appear to lose their force. One possible explanation for this is that the memory of past reinforcement becomes distorted. This is consistent with current theory and research in clinical psychology. This suggests that depression is associated with memory functions, whilst anxiety is associated with the functioning of perception.

The question remains, however, as to why depression, generally seen as an unpleasant experience, should continue for any length of time. A part of the answer would appear to be that, although depression is, by and large, unpleasant it does provide some benefits. First, it enables the individual to maintain a safe, and largely unassailable, view of the world. This consistency at least allows the individual the illusion of being able to predict what is likely to happen, even if what is going to happen will be bad. This prediction allows them the perception of control. Even though there may be nothing they can do to change negative events, at least they know what will happen. The second advantage is that it protects the individual against further experiences of the loss that initiates depression. If you take action and produce or acquire something, there is always the chance that this will also be lost. If you do nothing then nothing can be lost. Except in the most extreme cases, people eventually cease to self-focus in this way and, instead, direct their attention outwards. This has two effects. First, it removes the negative self-evaluative focus, and second, it focuses attention on the processing of information about the new reality.

During the *letting go* stage the individual realizes that the old behaviours will not lead to reinforcement. The testing stage, therefore, involves a search. Either new reinforcers have to be found or new behaviours have to be developed which will lead to a recovery of the original reinforcers. The *search for meaning* is more difficult to explain in behavioural terms, but then all the theories have their limitations, as well as their strengths. *Internalization*, however, can be seen as the integration of the new behaviour/reinforcement patterns.

Coping with change

The usefulness of the Hopson model is that it makes both individuals and organizations aware of the likely personal consequences of change. Just understanding this process has a value. Individuals realize that they are not alone in their experiences and feelings. They also become aware that each of the stages often fulfils a necessary function in the process of adapting to change. Organizations also need to recognize these elements of the change process and accept that different people will progress through the stages at different rates. But, whilst acceptance of the change process is useful, individuals and organizations can also take action help ease the passage through the stages.

Perhaps the most important advice that the behavioural approach can offer involves 'control' and 'self-efficacy'. Threat to perceived personal control is one of the common factors that appears throughout the literature on adaptation to change, whether in clinical, educational, or occupational psychology. To take an extreme case, one of the main problems of those suffering from 'post traumatic stress disorder' is loss of control. Those held hostage for a long time, for example, need help to re-establish control over their lives. It is not unusual for long-term hostages to even find it impossible to decide what to eat for their first meal of freedom. The 'de-briefing' often includes forcing them to take such, apparently simple, decisions. An acquaintance of one of the authors recounts how on leaving a monastic order, for the first few days he found life very difficult. It was a major effort to decide when to have lunch, and even more difficult to decide what to have. Control also has links with perceived self-efficacy. Those who believe they have control over their environment are more likely to have higher levels of self-efficacy.

Even in the more everyday work context, change (either personal or organizational) often means that new skills have to be acquired in order to cope. All the factors that were discussed in the discussion of social cognitive theory (see Chapter 4) will need to be taken into consideration. Suitable models will have to be developed. Skill acquisition will have to be arranged such that early failures are avoided and success encouraged. The new rewards that the changes will bring will have to be made clear. If possible intrinsic rewards should be built into the new working arrangements. These are matters for which the individual and the organization will need to take joint responsibility.

In our experience much change is, perhaps inevitably, driven from the top. However, it is only initial policy decisions regarding change that need to be made at this level. Decisions about the process and nature of the change should often be made lower down the organization. If it is not possible to give individuals actual control over their environment then they should at least be kept fully informed. Being informed allows people to make predictions. This, in itself, allows individuals a form of control.

Organizations should accept the fact that change takes time and that people should be supported and encouraged to help themselves. In particular, the reward system that encourages change should not be devised so as to encourage competition. Self-improvement goals are generally more effective than competitive goals when new skills are being acquired. Organizations, by their reward systems, can influence which of these goal orientations people will adopt. Rewards should be individually tailored so as to achieve high levels of self-development. As Wood and Bandura (1989) put it: 'To ensure progress in personal development, success should be measured in terms of self improvement, rather than triumphs over others'. In other words cooperation is better than competition.

Gaining cooperation or getting to win–win

Unfortunately, human beings often become very competitive, particularly in situations where they feel threatened. Competition will lead to low trust and, by definition, low cooperation. For example there is often rivalry and low trust between shifts and between shop floor and management. In most (although not necessarily all) such situations this leads to lowered effectiveness. It will certainly lead to a less than smooth introduction of change, whether via the behavioural approach or any other method. The situation will be made worse if there is suspicion concerning the activities of any consultants involved. It is important, therefore, to be aware of any signs of competition and to know how to deal with it, or better still know how to avoid it in the first place. There are a number of factors which determine how well people work together. These apply whatever the context. Three of them are of particular importance.

1 The extent to which people *trust* each other: the level of trust can vary from very high to very low.
2 How *open* people or groups are with each other: again openness can be high or low.
3 Whether there is *cooperation* or *competition*: there can be high cooperation or high competition.

All three of these factors can have significance for the relationship between the participants and whoever is implementing the scheme. They are also important aspects of the relationship between managers and subordinates in the organization. Depending on past experience of consultants there may be low trust in outside experts. It is also not uncommon for levels of trust between managers and workers on the shop floor to

153

be low. The issue is not only how much people believe what is said, but also how much confidence they have that others will deliver what they have promised. For a variety of reasons managers may not communicate openly and so subordinates feel that they are not getting the full story. Competition between different departments or shifts is also a common phenomenon in organizations. Obviously, for any change intervention to be effective, trust and openness should be high, which will lead to cooperation rather than competition.

A further complication is that the three factors interact with each other. If trust is low, people tend to be less open and do not communicate and so become suspicious of each other's motives, this leads to low cooperation or competition. This, in turn makes the participants more suspicious of each other and the interaction goes into a downward spiral (or vicious circle) of lowered trust and communication and increasing competition. This is a not uncommon experience in times of change in organizations. If trust is high people tend to be more open; this openness creates more interaction leading to greater trust, which in turn increases cooperation. This raises the level of trust still higher, leading to an upward spiral (or virtuous circle). In practice the best advice is to maintain, as far as possible, complete openness, as this is the best way to build trust and reduce competition.

In case it should be assumed that we are advocating a 'love and trust' model as a panacea for all ills, it is worth pointing out that we are not saying that openness and trust are appropriate in all situations and that one should always go for cooperation. To be a little technical for a moment, whether cooperation or competition is most appropriate depends on the *type of situation* – whether it is *zero sum* or *non zero sum*.

A *zero sum* situation is one where one person's losses are the other person's winnings and vice versa.

A *non-zero sum* situation is one where there is some outside influence which can add to, or subtract from, the total gains available.

In zero sum situations competition can be appropriate. In non-zero sum situations competition will always lead to both sides losing (lose–lose). Cooperation will lead to both sides winning (win–win). Most 'real life' situations are non-zero sum. If people cooperate, both sides gain. This applies to everything from war to trade union negotiations. In almost every industrial dispute that has reached the stage of strike action, both sides have lost more than was gained by the strike. In the final settlement, the strikers rarely recoup their losses in terms of lost pay, or if they do it takes a considerable time. Management also loses heavily in lost production and subsequent lost profits. If they could have cooperated and reached a quick agreement both sides could have gained. Similar considerations apply to change initiatives. If a spirit of cooperation can be maintained a successful conclusion can be reached quickly and with minimum cost. If low trust and competition develops, time is wasted and the whole project can be jeopardized.

Most real-life zero sum situations are relatively trivial. Gambling games between friends provide an example. (Gambling at casinos is usually non-zero sum, since there is often a slight built-in advantage towards the casino.) In these situations competition is appropriate. There is, in fact, little point in doing otherwise. However, our advice is not to get involved unless you are better at the game than the other person: otherwise you will surely lose. We know of no such situations within the work of organizations.

Staying OK

Whether the individuals involved in any project start off, and continue with, a positive, open and trusting relationship will depend to some extent on how they feel about each other. There is a framework which we have found helpful in this context. It is derived from the work of Franklin Ernst (1971) and is concerned with how you perceive other people. It is also involves attitude to others, but in this case, since we are referring to our own attitudes, it is possible to do something about them. It is part of a larger theory, but in this context we refer to the concept as *Staying OK*. In this framework the term 'OK' is used in a semi-technical way, but the meaning is much the same as when we use the expression in everyday life. If someone is seen as 'OK', then they have value as a person and their views and opinions have to be considered seriously. They are competent and are in control of their life. Someone who is seen as not 'OK' is, on the other hand, seen as the opposite of this. They do not seem to be in control, and their views and opinions can be dismissed without consideration. As a person they are of no consequence.

The concept of being 'OK' or 'Not OK' can be applied both to oneself and to others. Thus I can feel 'OK' or 'Not OK' and, likewise, can see you as 'OK' or 'Not OK'. This gives us the four positions shown in Figure 7.4. We will consider each of the four positions in turn. It is important to remember that these positions are *assumptions* that we are making about ourselves and about others. They do not, necessarily, reflect reality.

I'm OK You're Not OK	I'm OK You're OK
I'm Not OK You're Not OK	I'm Not OK You're OK

Figure 7.4 Staying OK

I'm OK, You're Not OK

If I'm OK, then I have value as a person and my ideas and views also have value. You, on the other hand, being Not OK have little or no value. Hence your views don't count and I can ignore them. In extreme cases I can get rid of you by, for example, firing you (or getting you fired). I will feel important and self-righteous, you will feel belittled and discounted.

I'm Not OK, You're OK

This is, in many ways, the reverse of the above position. Everyone else, but me, seems to be in control and know what they are doing. Whereas, I am completely confused and do not know what is going on. I feel worthless, while everyone else seems competent and valuable. In this situation, most people keep quiet and make no contribution, hoping that no one will notice them. In extreme cases they will leave the situation, either temporarily by walking out, or more permanently, by resigning.

I'm Not OK, You're Not OK

In this situation I do not know what is going on and no one else seems to either. We are all confused and since no one understands what is going on there is no way out of the mess we are in. I feel worthless and no one else is competent or of any value. Most people feel this way, at times, in most organizations, particularly in times of change.

I'm OK, You're OK

In this position I see myself as competent and in control, and see you as the same. We may have different views and beliefs, but I see yours to be equally as valid as my own. If we discuss and share ideas we may come to an agreement, or feel comfortably able to differ. Either way we will respect and value each other's views.

Hopefully, most people spend most of their time in ' I'm OK, You're OK', but most of us can recognize that there are times when we move off into one of the other positions. The commonest fallback position is, probably, ' I'm OK, You're Not OK'. This is certainly very common in organizations. The implication of this is that when things go wrong it is the other person's fault. The effect of communicating from this position is usually to push the other person into the same ' I'm OK, You're Not OK' position, so that you end up in an argument. It is worth considering what are your own favourite fallback positions, if you do move away from ' I'm OK, You're OK' and what are the implications of communicating from such a position. The important thing to remember is that the only effective position, from which to communicate is 'I'm OK, You're OK'.

Unfortunately, it is not uncommon for managers to work from I'm OK, you're Not OK, in relation to subordinates (or colleagues). Even more unfortunately the same can be true of trainers and consultants. It is obvious that this is not a good position to work from, as the other feels put down and belittled. Such an approach will inevitably generate antagonism and start the downward vicious spiral outlined above. It is, however all too easy to do. Both the Not OK positions in the lower half of Figure 7.4 are also, fairly obviously, not good places from which to work. Clearly, if openness, trust and cooperation are to be generated and maintained, it is essential to maintain a relationship characterized by I'm OK, you're OK.

CHAPTER SUMMARY

Points to be considered when specifying behaviour.

- Write down a brief description of the behaviour you want to change.
- Is what you have written a behaviour or an *outcome* of behaviour, e.g. a sales target?
    If so rewrite in behavioural terms, e.g. 'make at least *x* calls a week on potential customers'.
- Is what you have written a single behaviour or a *summary* of a number of behaviours, e.g. being a more considerate motorist?
    If it is a summary rewrite as a small number of specific behaviours, e.g. 'let at least one other driver into a traffic queue when traffic is slow moving'.
- Can the behaviour be observed, preferably by a third party?
- Would two people agree as to whether the behaviour was, or was not, occurring?
- Can you produce a baseline – either frequency or time?
- Will the behaviour produce the results you want?

From what we have said above it is clear that, when introducing change, some resistance is almost inevitable. It is quite natural that people will be doubtful when faced with something new and challenging, particularly if it is seen as making more work or life harder for them in some way. Also they may not, at first, perceive the potential benefits. Even when a benefit such as safer working conditions may seem to be of obvious value, they may not believe that it is attainable. For effective introduction of change it is necessary to understand and be sympathetic towards the reasons for any such resistance. Remember, if people are raising doubts or asking difficult questions, they may have a valid point and have seen a possible problem or, perhaps, a better way of doing things. There are a number of straightforward practical recommendations that we can make, which will help the introduction of such change.

- Be clear about what is entailed in the change and communicate effectively what is involved. Tell people what they are expected to do, how long it will take and what extra work is involved. Explain the benefits to be expected, i.e. a safer workplace.
- Remember that effective communication involves listening and encouraging questions and discussion.
- Be honest when introducing the scheme. Admit to the potential problems and costs and ask for suggestions to overcome them.
- Aim for cooperation not submission (i.e. inter-dependence not dependence).
- If people are raising objections or making suggestions, they may have a good point. Be prepared to listen to them and, if possible, adopt their ideas.
- Remember that change takes time. Don't expect everything to happen at once.
- For change to be effective it should be introduced and implemented in a positive atmosphere of cooperation.

References

Abramson, L.Y., Metalsky, G.I. and Alloy, L.B. (1989) 'Hopelessness depression: a theory-based subtype of depression'. *Psychological Review,* 96, 358–72.

Anderson, D., Crowell, C., Hantula, C.R. and Siroky, L.M. (1988) 'Task clarification and individual performance posting for improving cleaning in a student-managed university bar'. *Journal of Organizational Behavior Management,* 9(2), 73–90.

Argyris, C. (1962) *Interpersonal Competence and Organizational Effectiveness.* Homewood, IL: Dorsey.

Bandura, A. (1982) 'Self-efficacy mechanism in human agency'. *American Psychologist,* 37, 122–47.

Bandura, A. (1986) *Social Foundations of Thought and Action: A Social Cognitive Theory.* Englewood Cliffs, NJ: Prentice Hall.

Beck, A.T. (1976) *Cognitive Therapy and Emotional Disorders.* Harmondsworth: Penguin.

Berthold, H.C. (1982) 'Transitional contingency contracting and the Premack principle in business', in R. O'Brian, A. Dickinson and M. Roscow (eds), *Industrial Behaviour Modification: A Management Handbook.* New York: Pergamon.

Buchanan, D.A. and Huczynski, A.A. (1985) *Organizational Behaviour: An Introductory Text.* London: Prentice Hall.

Chesson, A.C. *et al.* (1999) 'Practice parameters for the nonpharmacologic treatment of chronic insomnia'. *Sleep,* 22(8), 1128–33.

Cooper, C.L. and Makin P.J. (1984) *Psychology for Managers.* London: Macmillan and The British Psychological Society.

Cullen, C. (1998) 'The trouble with rules', *The Psychologist.* October.

Cummings, T.G. and Huse, E.F. (1989) *Organization Development and Change* (4th edition). Saint Paul, MN: West Publishing.

Daniels, A.C. (1989) *Bringing out the Best in People.* New York: McGraw-Hill.

Dweck, C.S. (1999) *Self-Theories.* Philadelphia, PA: Psychology Press.

Eagly, A.H. and Chaiken, S. (1993) *The Psychology of Attitudes.* Fort Worth, TX: Harcourt Brace.

Ernst, F. (1971) 'The OK Corral: the grid for "get on with"'. *Transactional Analysis Journal,* 1, 4.

Festinger, L. (1957) *A Theory of Cognitive Dissonance.* Evanston, IL: Row Peterson.

Försterling, F. (1985) 'Attributional retraining: a review'. *Psychological Bulletin,* 98, 495–512.

Gray, J. (1991) *Beyond the New Right: Markets, Government and the Common Environment.* London: Routledge.

Hall, B. (1983) *OBM in Multiple Business Environments*. New York: Haworth Press.

Harrison, R. (1987) *Organization Culture and Quality of Service*. London: Association for Management Education and Development.

Homme, L. and Tosti, C. (1971) *Behaviour Technology: Motivation and Contingency Management*. San Rafael, CA: Individual Learning Systems.

Huczynski, A. and Buchanan, D. (1991) *Organizational Behaviour*. Harlow Prentice Hall.

Hutton, W. (1995) *The State We're In*. London: Cape.

Jaques, E. (1951) *The Changing Culture of a Factory*. London: Tavistock.

Kazdin, A.E. (1994) *Behavior Modification in Applied Settings*. Pacific Grove, CA: Dorsey.

Komaki, J.L. (1998) *Leadership from an Operant Perspective*. New York: Routledge.

Kubler-Ross, E. (1969) *On Death and Dying*. New York: Macmillan.

Leslie, J.C. and O'Reilly, M.E. (1999) *Behavior Analysis: Foundations and Applications to Psychology*. Amsterdam, The Netherlands: Harwood.

Likert, R. (1961) *New Patterns of Management*. New York: McGraw Hill.

Luthans, F. and Kreitner, R. (1985) *Organizational Behaviour Modification and Beyond*. Glenview, IL: Scott Foresman.

McGregor, D. (1960) *The Human Side of Enterprise*. New York: McGraw-Hill.

Malik, K. (2000) *Man, Beast and Zombie: What Science Can and Cannot Tell Us About Human Nature*. London: Weidenfeld and Nicolson.

Martin, G. and Pear, J. (1996) *Behavior Modification: What It Is and How To Do It* (5th edition). Englewood Cliffs, NJ: Prentice Hall.

Maslow, A.H. (1954) *Motivation and Personality*. New York: Harper & Row.

Maslow, A.H. (1971) *The Farther Reaches of Human Nature*. New York: Viking.

Mayo, E. (1975) *The Social Problems of an Industrial Civilisation*. London: Routledge & Kegan Paul.

Mintzberg, H. (1973) *The Nature of Managerial Work*, New York, Harper & Row.

Neck, C.P. and Manz, C.C. (1992) 'Thought self-leadership: the influence of self-talk and mental imagery on performance'. *Journal of Organizational Behaviour*, 13, 681–99.

Peale, N.V. (1990) *The Power of Positive Thinking*. New York: Simon & Schuster.

Peters, T.J. and Waterman, R.H. (1982) *In Search of Excellence*. New York: Harper & Row.

Quick, J.C. and Quick, J.D. (1984) *Organizational Stress and Preventative Management*. New York: McGraw-Hill.

Randell, G.A., Packard, P. and Slater, J. (1984) *Staff Appraisal* (3rd edition). London: Institute of Personnel Management.

Roethlisberger, F.J. and Dickson, W.J. (1939) *Management and the Worker*. Boston, MA: Harvard University Press.

Schein, E. (1984) 'Coming to a new awareness of organizational culture'. *Sloan Management Review*, 25, 3–16.

Seligman, M.E.P. (1975) *Helplessness: On Depression, Development and Death*. San Francisco: Freedman.

Seligman, M.E.P. (2003) *Authentic Happiness*. London: Nicholas Brealey.

Semler, R. (1994) *Maverick! The Success Story Behind the World's Most Unusual Workplace*. London: Arrow.

Stajkovic, A.D. and Luthans, F. (2001) 'Differential effects of incentive motivators on work performance'. *Academy of Management Journal*, 44 (3), 580–90.

Sutherland, V.J., Makin, P.J. and Cox, C.J. (2000) *The Management of Safety*. London: Sage.

Taylor, F.W. (1911) *The Principles of Scientific Management*. New York: Harper & Row.

Tversky, A. and Kahneman, D. (1974) 'Judgement under uncertainty'. *Science*, 85, 112–31.

Weiner, B. (1985) 'An attributional theory of achievement motivation and emotion'. *Psychological Review*, 92(4), 548–573.

Wilk, J. (1989) 'Culture and epistemology: media of corporate stability and strategic change'. *International Journal of Systems Research and Information Science*, 3, 143–67.

Wood, R., and Bandura, A. (1989) 'Social cognitive theory of organizational management'. *Academy of Management Review*, 14(3), 361–84.

Zaleznik, A. (1977) 'Managers and leaders: are they different?' *Harvard Business Review*, May/June.

Zenger, T.R. (1992) 'Why do employers only reward extreme performance? Examining the relationships among performance, pay and turnover'. *Administrative Science Quarterly* 37, 198–219.

Zohar, D. (2002) 'Modifying supervisory practices to improve subunit safety: a leadership-based intervention model'. *Journal of Applied Psychology*, 87: 156–63.

Zohar, D. and Fussfeld, N. (1981) 'A systems approach to organizational behaviour modification: theoretical considerations and empirical evidence'. *International Review of Applied Psychology*, 30: 491–505.

Index